Introduction

The units in this Workbook supplement and review those in the *First Language English for Cambridge IGCSE Student Book*. Each unit contains different sections focusing on language skills. The **Reading** sections contain a wide variety of texts, including blogs, news and feature articles, autobiography and fiction. After each passage there are exam-style questions. The **Using English** sections give the opportunity for grammar and spelling practice; there are also vocabulary and language awareness exercises to help you improve all your language skills. The **Writing** sections include useful information on writing **Compositions** and on **Directed Writing** tasks, where you are asked to read a passage and use that information to write in a specified style, for example a speech, interview, letter or article.

The Cambridge IGCSE® First Language English syllabus is designed to help you develop your ability to communicate clearly, accurately and effectively in both speech and writing. To this end, this Workbook will help you to develop a wider vocabulary and use grammar, spelling and punctuation more accurately in your written work. This will help you to communicate more appropriately and effectively; it will also influence your personal writing style for narrative and descriptive essays.

As you develop your reading skills, you will also be improving your analytical skills, learning how to analyse texts and infer implicit meanings and attitudes; how to order facts; and present opinions politely and effectively. All students preparing for English exams should try to read widely to improve their awareness of how English can be used for different purposes, for example, to inform or entertain. Reading stories from different English-speaking countries will broaden your vocabulary and cultural knowledge. Reading stories from different periods in time will show you how people thought, spoke and behaved in the past. Reading online newspapers will keep you up to date with what is happening in the world for class discussions or debates, discursive essays or coursework assignments. Reading widely helps you to become aware of register and how English is used in different contexts. It also helps you to develop the critical thinking skills needed in all school subjects.

1 Travellers' tales

Writing skills questionnaire

1. Tick the writing activities below that you like doing.

   ☐ Writing stories

   ☐ Descriptive writing (to inform and entertain)

   ☐ Writing informative or discursive essays (to argue a point)

   ☐ Writing History, Geography or Business Studies essays

   ☐ Writing up experiments

   ☐ Writing articles for the school magazine or English lessons

   ☐ Writing long emails to friends

   ☐ Writing playscripts

   ☐ Texting

   ☐ Keeping a diary or writing a blog

2. Write answers to the following questions about what and how you write.

   a. Think about what you write on a daily basis. Apart from essays for school, what else do you write most days?

   ....

b. Do you consciously change your style for different writing activities? Give an example.

....

c. Choose two styles of writing that you use and explain how they differ (e.g. texting and essays).

....

d. Now think about your thinking skills. Are you aware of thinking in different ways when you write? If the answer is 'yes', how and why does your way of thinking change?

....

....

e. What different writing styles do you need to use in school subjects other than English?

....

....

f. Are there any writing activities that you do at school that you expect to use after you leave school?

....

g. Look at the writing styles you ticked in question 1. Choose one you are good at and/or enjoy. Explain what you like about it.

....

....

h. Do you think you will ever write for pleasure after you leave school, college or university? Explain why or why not.

....

....

i. Why do you think you have to learn how to write in different styles in English lessons?

....

....

j. "Learning to write a good summary is the most useful skill you'll ever learn." Do you agree or disagree? Explain your thoughts.

....

....

....

....

....

Answering reading questions

Navigational dividers (n): a device like a compass used for making or calculating measurements at sea.

In this book, you will be asked to read passages of various lengths that have been written in different styles for a range of purposes. You will then be asked questions on the information they contain and on how the texts have been written.

Read the following passage carefully and answer the questions that follow.

Mystery of Alexander Selkirk, the real Robinson Crusoe, solved

By Richard Alleyne, *Daily Telegraph* (30 October 2008)

It may have taken nearly 300 years but archaeologists have finally confirmed the campsite of castaway Alexander Selkirk, thought to be the inspiration for Robinson Crusoe. 5

Scottish sailor Selkirk was marooned on a small tropical island in the Pacific for more than four years.

Cast away on a desert island, surviving on what nature alone can provide, praying for rescue but 10 at the same time fearing the sight of a boat on the horizon. These are the imaginative creations of Daniel Defoe in his famous novel *Robinson Crusoe*.

But the story is believed to be based on the real-life experience of Scottish sailor Selkirk, 15 marooned in 1704 on a small tropical island in the Pacific for more than four years, and now archaeological evidence has been found to support his existence on the island.

An article in the journal *Post-Medieval* 20 *Archaeology* claims that an archaeological dig on the Argentinian island of Aguas Buenas, 470 miles off the Chilean coast, reveals evidence of the campsite of an early European occupant. The most compelling evidence is the discovery 25 of a fragment of a pair of navigational dividers which could only have belonged to a ship's master or navigator, which historical evidence suggests Selkirk must have been.

Selkirk's rescuer, Captain Woodes Rogers' 30 account of what he saw on arrival at Aguas Buenas in 1709 lists "some practical pieces" and mathematical instruments amongst the few possessions that Selkirk had taken with him from the ship. 35

Dr David Caldwell, National Museums Scotland, who helped lead the dig, said the find finally confirmed the whereabouts of the castaway camp.

"The evidence uncovered at Aguas Buenas corroborates the stories of Alexander Selkirk's 40 stay on the island and provides a fascinating insight into his existence there," he said. "I am satisfied in my mind that this is the place where Selkirk set up his camp. I never thought we had a chance of finding it but the discovery of the 45 divider was crucial."

The finds also provide an insight into exactly how Selkirk might have lived on the island.

Postholes suggest he built two shelters near to a freshwater stream and had access to 50 a viewpoint over the harbour from where he would be able to watch for approaching ships and ascertain whether they were friend or foe. Accounts written shortly after his rescue describe him shooting goats with a gun rescued 55 from the ship and eventually learning to outrun them, eating their meat and using their skins as clothing.

[…] Alexander Selkirk was born in the small seaside town of Lower Largo, Fife, Scotland in 60 1676. A younger son of a shoemaker, he was drawn to a life at sea from an early age. In 1704, during a privateering voyage on the Cinque Ports, Selkirk fell out with the commander over the ship's seaworthiness and he decided to remain 65 behind on an island, now named Robinson Crusoe, where they had landed to overhaul the worm-infested vessel. He cannot have known that it would be five years before he was picked up by an English ship visiting the island. 70

1. Answer the following questions. Quote from the text to support your answers where necessary.

   a. Identify and describe the "compelling evidence" mentioned in line 25.

   ....

   ....

   ....

   ....

   ....

   b. Give another word or phrase the writer could have used instead of "compelling" in line 25.

   ....

   ....

   ....

   ....

   ....

   c. Explain why this evidence is "compelling".

   ....

   ....

   ....

   ....

   ....

   d. In line 46 the writer says the discovery of the "divider was crucial". Explain why.

   ....

   ....

   ....

   ....

   e. Identify another "find" (line 47) that was important to the archaeologists.

   ....

   ....

   ....

   ....

2. Using the article on Alexander Selkirk for information, complete the chart below.

Alexander Selkirk	Information in the text
Where he came from	
Biographical details	
Where he was marooned	
What he had with him on the island	
How he passed his time	
His rescue	
Other interesting details	

Answering summary questions

Answering summary questions gives you the opportunity to demonstrate both your reading and writing skills.

Here is some guidance on how to begin.

a. Keyword the question. For example, complete the keywording that has been started below.

> **Summarise the conditions and the evidence found on Aguas Buenas Island that may explain how Alexander Selkirk survived there alone for four years.**

b. Re-read the whole passage on page 6 and identify information that is relevant to the question. (You may only need certain paragraphs, not the whole passage.) Annotate the text as you go along to help you to locate information later. Some examples are given below. Look at how one student has found, deduced and labelled information.

Cast away on a desert island, surviving on what nature alone can provide, praying for rescue but at the same time fearing the sight of a boat on 5 the horizon. These are the imaginative creations of Daniel Defoe in his famous novel *Robinson Crusoe*.

But the story is believed 10 to be based on the real-life experience of Scottish sailor Selkirk, marooned in 1704 on a small tropical island in the Pacific for more than four years, 15 and now archaeological evidence has been found to support his existence on the island.

An article in the journal *Post-Medieval Archaeology* 20 claims that an archaeological dig on the Argentinian island of Aguas Buenas, 470 miles off the Chilean coast, reveals evidence of the campsite of an early 25 European occupant…

> tropical – so probably had fruit and berries, and not very cold at night

> lived off the land (and sea) – Aguas Buenas (good water?)

> wood to make a fire

c. In the passage on page 6 there are eight significant points on Alexander Selkirk and how he may have survived on Aguas Buenas Island. Organise the eight points below so they directly answer the question. You can do this by numbering them.

- ....
- ....
- ....
- ....
- ....
- ....
- ....
- ....

d. Now write out the significant points concisely to summarise how Alexander Selkirk may have survived for over four years alone on Aguas Buenas Island. Your summary should contain all eight points in your notes.

Use your own words as far as possible and continuous writing (not note form). Write no more than 120 words. Use a separate sheet of paper if necessary.

....
....
....
....
....
....
....
....
....
....
....
....
....
....
....
....
....
....
....
....
....
....
....
....
....
....
....
....

Descriptive writing (1)

Here are two descriptions of riverside settings: one is in Australia, the other in England. Read the descriptions below carefully, then do the descriptive writing activity that follows.

Passage A: New South Wales, Australia, 1813

By the time the sun was lighting up the topmost leaves of the forest, he was away a ways up the valley. It was a still and silent place. The water, although clear, was as brown as strong tea. On either side mangroves masked the banks. Beyond was a narrow strip of level ground where river-oaks hung, and then the ridges   5
angled up, steep and stony on either side.

    The mosquitoes were ferocious. Thornhill watched a big one with striped legs land on his arm and push its needle-like biting part against the stuff of his shirt until it bent. Somewhere ahead of him at the top of a tree, a bird made a measured silvery sound   10
again and again, a little bell being struck. A fish launched itself out of the water and through the air in a flash of silver muscle. The place held its breath, watching.

From *The Secret River*, by Kate Grenville (2005)

Passage B: Cornwall, England, 1913

A roll of thick white mist curled around the many cornered house, sidled up the chimneys and settled down to await the sun. Below, between high willow herb and tall rushes, the old river barely moved. A late night water rat cut his way home through the shallows. An early rising trout snapped a fly. Along the waterside,   5
the never quiet ducks pattered and chattered. Coots gathered food among the reeds. A heron speared an unwary amphibian for breakfast. Morning had come to a slow turn in a Tamar valley.

From *The Empress Emerald*, by J.G. Harlond (2016)

Coot: a small, dark grey water bird with a white mark on its head.

1. Write a paragraph describing a peaceful place. Use the planning grid below to help you.

   Include the following information.
   - Where: setting and a description of the place
   - When: the time of day
   - Who: presence or absence of people
   - How: imagery and figurative language (simile/metaphor)
   - Effect: how you see or imagine each place

Setting	
Time	
People	
Imagery	
Figurative language	
Desired effect(s) on reader	

2. Write a paragraph describing a tranquil place you know (it does not have to be near a river). Include the following:
   - setting (time and place)
   - atmosphere
   - descriptive imagery.

   Write between 350 and 450 words by hand. Use a separate sheet of paper if necessary. This is good practice for your exams.

REMINDER

Remember to use your five senses in descriptive writing. Think about how you want your reader to interpret what you have written.

....
....
....
....
....
....
....
....
....
....
....
....

2 The world of nature

Reading skills questionnaire

1. Look at the following types of text and think about the ways you might read them.

Type of text	Active reading	Passive reading
Clocks		
Ingredients listed on a food product label		
Cereal packets on the breakfast table		
Recipes		
Mobile phone texts		
Instructions for your mobile phone		
First page of a novel		
Email from a friend		
Exam questions		
Newspaper headlines		
Magazines in waiting rooms		
Interesting blog posts		

2. Which of the above texts require active reading skills, where you have to read each word or item of data carefully? Tick them in the 'Active reading' column.

3. Which texts can you read passively, without thinking about what you are reading too much? Tick them in the 'Passive reading' column.

Remember that you can read some texts both ways, depending on the situation or your level of interest.

Improving reading skills

Good reading skills are essential for success in English. Through reading you can understand how and why a text was written and this will help you to develop and improve your own writing skills. Even passive reading improves vocabulary, grammar and your speaking and listening skills. Active reading improves life skills and will therefore help you in all your school subjects.

You can use different levels of reading according to what you need to know. You may glance through a magazine and skim titles, headlines or subheadings until you find something of interest; then, depending how much you want to know or how challenging the vocabulary is, you read the actual text with a greater level of attention. In exams with a choice of question, you probably skim through the questions until you find one you can answer well and then read the instructions for that question carefully to understand what you need to do.

Skimming and scanning

Skimming is reading quickly to get the gist of what a text is about. Your eye skims words and illustrations to give you an idea of what it is about.

Scanning is reading to locate specific information or details.

Close reading and keywording questions

Once you have chosen your question in an exam, it is vital to re-read it very carefully. You need to understand precisely what you are being asked to do: keyword the question by selecting the important (key) words that tell you what to do and what to include in your answer.

Close reading and analysing texts

You also need to use close reading skills to analyse texts to find out how they have been written.

Close reading is sometimes called textual analysis because it examines the writer's style, vocabulary and use of language and analyses the effects on the reader. For example, when you think about advertisements, ask yourself: How has the advertiser tried to influence me?

Scanning

Read this article about animals in danger of extinction and do the reading activities that follow.

Gorillas, monkeys and lemurs face "impending extinction"

By Ian Johnston, *The Independent* (18 January 2017)

Research by thirty-one leading scientists published in the journal *Science Advances* demonstrates scores of different species of primates, monkeys and lemurs are facing "impending extinction".

Primates are still hunted for meat and body parts and some are captured for pets, but the single greatest threat to their survival comes from increased industrial-scale farming for foodstuffs such as palm oil. Other threats come from the building of dams, mining, and oil and gas exploration, which also bring the spread of human diseases to which these animals are susceptible. About 60 per cent of the 504 primate species investigated are threatened with extinction. 75 per cent have declining populations. [15]

Researchers insist they can only be saved if immediate action is taken. "Unless we act, human-induced environmental threats in primate range regions will result in a continued and accelerated reduction in primate biodiversity," the scientists said. Entire primate groups are at risk from "a combination of habitat loss and degradation", [20] plus the dangers from hunting and trapping. Rapid population decline in some areas is due to human and domestic animal-borne diseases, and increasing human encroachment. [25]

Illinois Professor Paul Garber, who co-led the study with Alejandro Estrada of the National Autonomous University of Mexico, emphasises how close extinction is for some iconic species saying, [30] "This truly is the eleventh hour for many of these creatures."

The ring-tailed lemur, Udzunga red colobus monkey, Yunnan snub-nosed monkey, white-headed langur and Grauer's gorilla are down to a [35] few thousand individuals. Fewer than 30 Chinese Hainan gibbons are left in the wild. The critically endangered Sumatran orang-utan lost 60 per cent of its habitat between 1985 and 2007.

"Agricultural practices are disrupting and [40] destroying vital habitat for 76 percent of all primate species on the planet," Professor Garber said. "Sadly, in the next 25 years, many of these primate species will disappear unless we make conservation a global priority." [45]

Scan the article about endangered animals to complete the sentences below. Use numbers only, and the % sign where relevant. The first one has been done for you.

a. Between 1985 and 2007 Sumatran orang-utans lost ....*60%*.... of their habitat.

b. Of the .... primate species that were investigated, ... have declining populations.

c. Agriculture is negatively affecting .... of all primate species on our planet.

d. .... named species are down to a few thousand individuals and there are fewer than .... Hainan gibbons left in China.

e. We must prioritise conservation across the world or many primates will disappear in the next .... years.

Improving summarising skills

When summarising information we have heard, read or been told verbally, we often generalise. However, it is not always possible to generalise facts, times or important data, so we sometimes need to include them as concisely as possible.

Re-read the text about animals in danger on page 15. Summarise which animals are in danger of extinction and what can be done to prevent it.

1. Find relevant information and make brief notes in the margin. Include:

    *   which species have rapidly declining populations
    *   why they are facing extinction
    *   the principal causes of these threats
    *   what needs to be done to remedy the situation.

2. Write out a rough version of the main points.

....

....

....

....

....

3. Write your summary. You must use continuous writing, not notes. Write no more than 120 words in clear, neat handwriting.

....

....

....

....

....

....

....

....

....

....

....

....

....

....

....

....

Improving narrative writing skills

Writing compositions is your opportunity to demonstrate your knowledge of different writing styles, your personal writing skills (including use of English and vocabulary) and your technical accuracy (grammar and spelling).

1. Read the following points on how to write good **narrative compositions**. Then choose one of the questions on the next page.

    *   Choose a question you will enjoy writing and/or you can do well.

    *   Read and keyword the question carefully. You may have to include certain words or write only the beginning or end of a story.

    *   Even if you only have to write an episode or the beginning of a story, plan your storyline and decide how the episode ends before you begin. The end of a story may come as a surprise to the reader, but the writer should know exactly what is going to happen. A good narrative builds up to a climax and leads towards a conclusion.

    Some good stories start with a framing device such as a frightening flashback or someone telling the story to listeners, but do not attempt this if it is not appropriate to the question or could confuse the reader. Never end a story with *and then I woke up* or *It was all a dream*.

    *   If you are writing an episode, the beginning or the end of a story, you do not need a beginning/middle/end format.

    *   Keep the storyline simple but try to vary the pace of the narrative: if it is too slow, it will become boring; too fast, and it will become confusing.

    *   Decide on the tense you are going to use. Narrative compositions are usually written in the past tense, but can also be written in the present tense.

    *   Decide on the narrative voice (who is telling the story), whether you want to write in the first person (*I/we*) or third person (*he/she/it*). Do not change the narrative viewpoint (voice) once you have begun.

    *   Keep the number of characters to a minimum to avoid confusion. Bring characters and places to life with interesting details so the reader can imagine them in his or her mind's eye.

    *   Not all characters need dialogue. Too much dialogue will turn the story into a play so avoid giving characters trivial things to say. Indent dialogue like starting a new paragraph and punctuate direct speech accurately. Also find alternatives for *he/she said*.

    *   Use figurative language in your description with interesting metaphors and similes. Avoid over-used comparisons and clichés.

    *   Proofread and edit your composition. Silly mistakes ruin any form of writing. Professional authors write numerous drafts and edit them carefully. In an exam you do not have time to do this, but you must always leave time to read through and correct what you have written before it is handed in.

2. Write between 350 and 450 words on **one** of the following:

"Lost and alone" Write a story about being entirely on your own in a strange or unknown place. Write in the first person (*I*).

OR

Write the end of a story where the main character returns home after being away for a long period of time. Include the words "Home at last!". Write in the third person (*he/she/it*).

Use a separate sheet of paper if necessary.

....
....
....
....
....
....
....
....
....
....
....
....
....
....
....
....
....
....
....
....
....
....
....
....
....
....
....
....
....

Improving descriptive writing skills (2)

You may choose to write a narrative (see page 17) or a descriptive composition (see page 11) in the Paper 2 exam. Component 3, the coursework portfolio, requires you to write in both styles for Assignments 2 and 3.

1. Read the following points on how to write good **descriptive compositions**. Then answer the question that follows.

   A descriptive composition is not a story; it does not need a beginning, middle and an end. Give your description a framework, such as a clear setting or location in time, to create a structure, but do not create a storyline. If you are writing about a street market, for instance, you can be walking through the market or watching from an outdoor café, but you do not need to invent a dramatic incident.

   • Write about something you know well or have seen or felt in detail.

   • Use interesting, unusual vocabulary and a variety of sentence structures. For example, be precise when you describe colour: red can be blood-red or bright scarlet; green can be sea-green, apple-green or the colour of new-mown grass. Don't repeat words: find synonyms or alternative ways to express what you are seeing, thinking or feeling.

   • Try to use all five senses to give the reader a clear sense of the location, event and/or atmosphere. Include interesting, unusual or amusing details.

   • Avoid using clichés or overused, childish vocabulary such as *nice*, *little*, *old*, *big*, *good*, *bad*. Descriptive writing gives you a chance to show off your vocabulary, so use it!

2. Read the passage below about a rain storm in India.

Rain!

As it does every year, the wind has blown steadily out of the south-west, rolling its cargo of doughy air across the plain to slap hard against the mountains. For days, weeks, the air has funnelled upwards, cooling as it rises, spinning vast towers of condensation over the peaks. Now these hanging gardens of cloud have ripened to the point where they can no longer maintain themselves.

So, the rain.

It falls first over the mountains, an unimaginable shock of water. Caught in the open, herdsmen and woodcutters pull their shawls over their heads and run for shelter. Then in a chain reaction, cloud speaking to cloud, the rain rolls over the foothills, dousing fires, battering on roofs, bringing smiles to the faces of the people who run outside to greet it, the water for which they have been waiting so long.

From *The Impressionist*, by Hari Kunzru (2003)

3. Write about rain, a rainy day or the absence of rain in your country.

   Make your composition as descriptive as possible by using the five senses. Write between 350 and 450 words. Use a separate sheet of paper if necessary.

Points of view

Looking for evidence

Read the extract on the following pages from the historical novel *Catching the Eagle* by Karen Charlton, published in 2014, then answer the questions that follow.

The story is based on what happened to one of the author's family members in 1809 and is set in a rural area of Northumberland in northern England. In this scene a detective from London named Stephen Lavender and his assistant, Police Constable Woods, visit the cottage of a day labourer named Jamie Charlton. They are investigating the theft of over a thousand pounds in cash and paper bills from Kirkley Hall. Charlton, who was working at the Hall on the day of the robbery, is suspected of taking the money.

13 April 1809

The trap drew up outside Charlton's stone cottage. They could see it was a modest home of only a couple of rooms, with an overgrown garden to the front. The budding stems and brown thorns of a climbing rose clambered up the wall beside the partially open door. A spiral of smoke curled away from the chimney into the clear blue sky above. The delightful smell of freshly baked bread wafted in their direction.

"Well, at least there's someone at home," Woods observed.

They climbed down stiffly from the swaying vehicle, and sent a flurry of chickens squawking along the dusty track and onto the rickety fence which surrounded the tangled garden. In the tumbling confusion of daffodils, herbs, currant bushes and vegetables, a child's face suddenly appeared, framed with red curls and a dirty white bonnet. Seconds later, up popped another – identical to the last. Both girls were wide-eyed, and kneeling amongst the plants.

"What devil's trick is this!" the constable exclaimed.

Lavender smiled.

"Unusual isn't it? Twins rarely survive the birth. Is your father at home, little miss?"

The child did not answer. Behind her, the gaping door swung open and a tall, very beautiful woman was framed in the doorway. She wiped her floury hands on her apron and pushed back a wisp of gleaming, copper-coloured hair which had escaped from beneath her cap. Her large, green eyes flicked nervously across the faces of the two strange men before her.

"Are you wanting to see Jamie?" she asked.

"Mistress Charlton?" Lavender asked pleasantly. She nodded.

"We're looking for your husband, James Charlton. Is he at home?"

"He be out in the fields. Hannah, Mary – go fetch your da."

The two girls needed no second bidding. They were up from their knees in a second, flew out of the gate and sped off towards the fields. Their boots clattered over the stony path and red pigtails streamed behind them.

"Pretty gals, them," Woods observed.

"I'm Detective Lavender from Bow Street in London, Mistress Charlton. This is Constable Woods. We are investigating the theft of the rent money from Kirkley Hall."

"You'd better come inside then," Cilla said calmly.

They followed her into the cottage. Lavender was keen to have a good look around before Charlton arrived.

The door led straight into the main living area, which was dominated by the stone fireplace and a wooden table in the centre of the room. There was one padded armchair in front of the fire. At the other side of the hearth stood an ancient yew settle, scattered with colourful homemade cushions. A soot-blackened rag rug lay on the floor. Along the entire back wall of the room was an oak dresser crammed and cluttered with pots, pans, baking ingredients, knitting and sewing equipment and just about everything else the family owned. The table was covered with an appetising array of freshly made bread, pies and pastries.

Sitting on one of the wooden chairs at the table was a thin-faced woman who rose hurriedly as they entered.

"I'd best be getting along," she said.

"Take these into the bedroom, will you, Mary?" Cilla said quietly, ignoring her friend's embarrassment. She scooped up a pile of bulky brown paper parcels from the dresser and deposited them into the other woman's arms.

The woman pushed open the door on the back wall with her foot and carried the parcels away. For a brief second, Lavender was able to see several beds in the darkened room. A man's coat hung on the outside of a wardrobe door.

Cilla now began to move the food from the table into the space created on the dresser.

Lavender observed her dispassionately as she glided around the room. The faded blue dress she wore beneath her apron had lines of needle marks running from the dark stains beneath her armpits 90 down to her waist. It had obviously been let in and out several times – probably to accommodate her expanding waistline during pregnancies. As if on cue, an infant whimpered in the back room. She paused and listened but the sleepy child 95 seemed to settle again.

The woman was stunningly attractive but even in the darkened kitchen of the cottage he could see the fine lines around her eyes and the hint of grey at her temples. This magnificent red-headed 100 beauty was starting to lose her looks. How old would she be? Thirty perhaps? She was past her prime. Another five years of child-bearing, and the poverty and malnutrition which dogged her class would age her prematurely. 105

The woman Mary reappeared from the bedroom and moved towards the front door. She reached for her shawl from the back of the chair. Lavender and Woods stepped out of her way.

"I'll be seeing you, Cilla," she said as she left. 110 "Thank you for the money for the butter – I'll get you some change for that note as soon as I can." With this she gave Lavender and Woods a filthy look and then disappeared out of the cottage door.

Cilla gestured the men towards the spindly 115 chairs at the table.

"Take a seat," she said. "Jamie'll not be long; he's close by."

Lavender sat down and began to remove his gloves. He continued to scan the room. He saw 120 nothing unusual for a labourer's cottage: second-hand furniture, patched furnishings and pewter plates. There was another door off the kitchen which led to a small scullery. Cilla carried her baking implements into this side room [...]. 125

This family eats well at the moment, he thought.

"Can I get you a cup of tea?" Cilla asked when she returned. The two men accepted and watched as she picked up a teaspoon and a battered, tin tea caddy. She measured out the 130 leaves carefully then dropped them into a chipped, brown teapot. Next she reached for the iron kettle which sat on the hearthstones and set it back over the fire to boil.

Suddenly, they heard voices and footsteps in 135 the garden outside. The light in the cottage dimmed as a tall, broad man paused into the doorway.

"Good morning, Mr. Charlton. I'm Detective Lavender from Bow Street in London. I've come 140 to ask you some questions about your movements on the day of the Kirkley Hall robbery."

From *Catching the Eagle*, by Karen Charlton (2014)

Tea caddy: a container for tea leaves.

1. You are Detective Lavender. You think it is very probable that Jamie Charlton stole the money from Kirkley Hall. From memory, write down three items of evidence from the passage to suggest Charlton needs money.

   a. ....

   b. ....

   c. ....

2. You are Constable Woods. While you are at the cottage you make a list of evidence to suggest the Charlton family has recently acquired money. Re-read the passage and write down at least three points that demonstrate that Charlton has more money to spend than most poor folk in the area.

   ....

   ....

   ....

   ....

   ....

3. In those days a theft such as this was a hanging offence. Detective Lavender and Constable Woods need to be very sure of their facts before Charlton can be sent for trial. Is there any evidence in the passage to suggest Charlton may be innocent? Explain your thoughts.

   ....

   ....

   ....

4. You are Detective Lavender. Write a report for your superior in London explaining what you have seen at Charlton's cottage and why you want to stay in the area to make more enquiries. Write between 200 and 300 words. Use a separate sheet of paper if necessary.

   Start like this:

   Report on Kirkley Hall robbery, Northumberland,
   14 April 1809
   On the 13 April, the home of James Charlton was visited prior to his interrogation.

   It is evident from this visit that...

   ....

   ....

   ....

   ....

   ....

   ....

Using English: register

Register is the word for the style of language you use in a given situation or for a particular subject matter.

Decide whether the register in each of the following sentences is formal, neutral or informal.

	Formal	Neutral	Informal
a. There's this kid called Joey see and he's hanging around waiting for a bus.			
b. Further to my letter dated 13 November, I request once again that you review the situation regarding our invoice.			
c. "Now, I would like everyone to take a seat and listen carefully to what I'm going to say."			

Using English: informal to formal

Rewrite these informal sentences in a more formal register. Make use of the verb in brackets in your sentence in the appropriate tense: past, present or future.

1. It was Tom that did all the graffiti, but they're going to let him off this time if he cleans it all off himself. (to punish)

    ....

    ....

2. Tom's been made to say sorry for the mess he's made of the wall. (to apologise)

    ....

    ....

3. Jim's dad says he'll make Jim learn a useful trade if he doesn't get a job as soon as he leaves school. (to force)

    ....

    ....

4. My parents never let me stay up late on school nights. (to permit)

    ....

    ....

5. My mum says I have to help out with the housework if I want pocket money. (to oblige)

    ....

    ....

Improving directed writing skills: points of view

In Directed Writing or your Coursework Portfolio you are asked to demonstrate that you know how to write clearly, accurately and effectively in an argumentative, persuasive or discursive style. Many of the guidelines for writing in these styles also apply to participating in a debate, giving a persuasive speech or giving an informative talk.

Read the following advice on argumentative and discursive writing. Then choose one of the questions that follow.

Argumentative writing

In an argumentative letter or article, or a persuasive speech, you take a particular point of view and argue the case, demonstrating why you think it is the best. To strengthen your argument it is important to show that you have considered both sides of the argument. A balanced approach, giving the counter-arguments, is often a good way of highlighting the flaws in opposing points of view and adding credibility to your own. Plan your writing so that weak arguments and/or opposing views come first.

Discursive writing

A discursive letter or article is more informative: you discuss a range of possible views and then, if appropriate, outline your own thoughts on the subject.

Features of both styles

- You need a concise, effective introduction to capture the reader's attention and make the topic clear.

- Using personal pronouns (*I*, *you* and *we*) makes your writing more effective, but avoid getting too passionate or personal. This will make you sound over-emotional and subjective, and therefore less convincing.

- For argumentative or discursive writing in an exam, read, re-read and keyword the question carefully. There is often a single word in the question that affects the nature or emphasis of the argument. Underline words such as *obligatory*, *compulsory* or *always*.

- Think about the subject of the writing and plan carefully. Check the question and your plans as you go along to ensure your paragraphs have a logical structure and do not drift off the topic.

- Write the number of the question and/or a title.

- Never start paragraphs with *firstly*, *secondly*, *thirdly*. Use linking words that lead from one aspect of your argument to the next, for example: *furthermore*, *on the other hand*, *nevertheless*.

- Avoid using rhetorical questions and never end with a question such as: *So, what do you think?*

- Find an interesting, convincing way to close the writing. Avoid weak endings such as *to sum up* and *in conclusion*.

Find an article in the news or in a blog about the older generation, or the changing role of teachers or parents nowadays, and print it out.

Using information in this text, write an article for a magazine in either a discursive or argumentative style.

If you are preparing for Paper 2, write between 250 and 350 words. If you are preparing for Component 3, write between 500 and 800 words. Use a separate sheet of paper if necessary.

Use the discursive/argumentative planning outline on page 29 to help you plan your article before you write the final version. Plan each paragraph carefully. Construct your argument or set out your ideas in a logical sequence so each paragraph contains a clear topic sentence that leads to a conclusion. Give your article a title. Here are two ideas to get you started:

a. "Teachers shouldn't try to be friends or role models."

b. "It's natural and right that the older generation should tell young people what to do. Older people have the experience to know what is right and wrong."

....
....
....
....
....
....
....
....
....
....
....
....
....
....
....
....
....
....
....
....
....

PLAN
Title:
Introduction – explain exactly what you are going to discuss
Statement – say what you think or believe
Topic 1 – show both sides of the argument and give examples
Example 1
Example 2
Transition
Topic 2 – if necessary, examine another aspect of what people think and give examples
Example 1
Example 2
Transition
Topic 3 – demonstrate that your argument or analysis is valid
Final example – a concluding example that defeats your opponent's viewpoint or justifies your analysis
Conclusion

4 "All the world's a stage"

Exploring the writer's craft

In this passage from her autobiography *At the Source: A Writer's Year* (2008), Welsh author and poet Gillian Clarke describes nature in terms of theatre or a film. Read the passage and answer the questions that follow.

A wildlife spectacle

Paragraph 1

A flashback to kites falling on flesh. They appear out of the blue, at first just one or two specks in the sky, then more, until they are soaring in from all points over the mountains. Two or three hundred red kites firing in the sun as they flex and turn, homing down to a farm near Rhayader in mid-Wales. There, in a small field, fresh, raw meat is tipped from a trailer at the same hour every day. Diversification in agriculture has rarely been so imaginatively conceived. This is theatre.

Paragraph 2

Once the news is out, every kite in the mountain heartland of Wales knows it. The day in spring when I visit, a BBC camera team is preparing to film. Iolo Williams, 'the bird man', here to present the programme, tells me it is very likely that our kites from seventy miles away in Ceredigion are among these visitors, and that kites come to the feeding site from as far away as Yorkshire. How do they know? Do they have mobile phones?

Paragraph 3

First come the crows, minesweepers clearing the ground for the great arrival. Then the buzzards, outriders taking the risk to get a first snatch at the feast. Once the crows and buzzards have retreated to the trees with their share of flesh, and the lie of the

5

10

15

land looks safe, the first kite appears, distantly floating on the   20
thermals above the mountains. According to the farm's website,
on rare occasions, during strange weather maybe, the crows and
the buzzards have failed to arrive to feed. On those days the kites
eye the ground from afar but come no closer. But today all is well.
Crow and buzzard descend and fly off, then singly, in twos, tens,   25
hundreds, the angelic host blazes down on a field of blood.

***

Paragraph 4

Now it is August, and here, over our fields, seventy miles
south-west of that spectacular daily event, kites are a common
sight these days. This scavenger of the streets of medieval London
was persecuted, shot by gamekeepers, its nests plundered by egg   30
collectors until it was Britain's rarest bird. A few birds survived
in its heartland in the mountains of mid-Wales, though at worst,
according to reports of studies using DNA evidence, its numbers
were reduced to the offspring of a single female.

Paragraph 5

The other day a huge combine harvester was at work in our   35
neighbour's big barley field. All day, as the monstrous machine
growled up and down the field, four kites haunted the sky, causing
consternation to the buzzards and a crowd of crows competing to
feed on fresh kill: crushed mice, voles, rabbits, frogs.

Paragraph 6

A kite is a parable of beauty and violence. Its obsession, its   40
golden eye burning the ground for blood, the unflinching instinct
to survive. Riding the thermals, it flexes its wings and long forked
tail in independent movements – the only bird which can do that –
flaunting its auburns, manoeuvring the wind. As it drops on injured
prey or carrion it scarcely touches the ground. Such lazy grace,   45
such beauty, such savagery!

Paragraph 7

A ewe died deep in the gorse last winter, too far inside the thicket
to be discovered except by foxes and crows. Gorse makes a fortified
city, arched, aisled and alley-wayed for fox and badger or an old
sheep seeking respite from wind and rain. The kite circled, waiting,   50
while the crows and the buzzards ripped open the carcase. Then
it descended in slow, elegant circles, fell on the body, and gorged.
Flamboyance – that's the word I want, flame on air – its reds all
the more fiery against the clean bow of white under the span of its
wings, the black bars on its tail. Beautiful, gorging, gorgeous.   55

From *At the Source: A Writer's Year*, by Gillian Clarke (2008)

Kite (n): a large bird of prey.

Minesweeper (n): ships used for
clearing away explosive mines in
the sea.

Buzzard (n): a bird of prey.

1. Match each of the following headings to one of the paragraphs in the passage. One has been done for you.

   a. Warfare ....

   b. Background history ....

   c. Anecdote 1 ....

   d. Paradox ....

   e. Anecdote 2 ....

   f. Spectacle ....1..................................

2. In your own words explain how and why the author uses the following words and expressions. Use a dictionary to help you.

   a. "A flashback" (line 1)

   ....

   ....

   b. "homing down to a farm" (lines 4–5)

   ....

   ....

   c. "This is theatre." (line 8)

   ....

   ....

   d. "the lie of the land looks safe" (lines 19–20)

   ....

   ....

   e. "causing consternation" (lines 37–8)

   ....

   ....

   f. "a crowd of crows" (line 38)

   ....

   ....

   g. "A kite is a parable of beauty and violence." (line 40)

   ....

   ....

   h. "a fortified city" (lines 48–9)

   ....

   ....

i. "Flamboyance" (line 53)

....

....

j. "Beautiful, gorging, gorgeous." (line 55)

....

....

3. Using your own words as far as possible, explain how and why the author uses literary features to describe birds in mid-Wales.

a. Give two examples of metaphor and explain how they are used.

....

....

....

b. Give two examples of paradox or oxymoron and explain the author's choice of words.

....

....

....

c. Give two examples of alliteration and explain the effects.

....

....

....

d. Give one example of visual imagery and explain the author's choice of words.

....

....

....

e. Give one example of aural (or auditory) imagery and explain the author's choice of words.

....

....

....

Using English: proverbs and clichés

A **proverb** is a popular saying often expressed in a clever, brief way.

A **cliché** is an over-used expression that has been repeated so often it has lost its originality and in some cases its original meaning.

1. Read the following proverbs and explain what they mean in your own words.

   a. The early bird catches the worm.

   ....

   ....

   b. Absence makes the heart grow fonder.

   ....

   ....

   c. A stitch in time saves nine.

   ....

   ....

   d. Don't count your chickens until they're hatched.

   ....

   ....

   e. Empty vessels make the most noise.

   ....

   ....

2. Many proverbs have become so common that we only need to quote half or part of them for someone to understand what we are trying to say. Try to complete the following examples.

   a. There's no smoke ....

   b. A bird in the hand ....

   c. A friend in need ....

   d. Nothing ventured ....

   e. Too many cooks ....

3. Some popular expressions have become so over-used that they are now clichés. Using clichés in your writing shows a lack of imagination.

Find interesting, original ways to finish the following similes.

a. As good as ....

b. As black as ....

c. It'll spread like ....

d. These will sell like ....

e. He's as strong as ....

4. Tick the comparisons that, in your opinion, are now clichés.

a. Like a fish out of water ☐

b. Like a headless chicken ☐

c. Like greased lightning ☐

d. Like a bull in a china shop ☐

e. Like there's no tomorrow ☐

5. Find more interesting and imaginative ways to say each of the following examples.

a. Having a whale of a time

....

b. On cloud nine

....

c. Keeping a low profile

....

d. Out in the sticks

....

e. Lost to the world

....

5 Family and friends

Interpreting the meaning of new words

You may encounter words and phrases that are new to you in the passage below. Try to answer the questions that follow by looking at the context of the words. Do not use a dictionary or thesaurus to check your understanding of the words until you have completed the final question.

This first passage is from the autobiography of Mineko Iwasaki, a retired Japanese geisha. A geisha is a woman who has received rigorous training from childhood to sing and dance in the classical Japanese style. Mineko is explaining something of her father's family history.

Peerage: the nobility; high-ranking members of society.

Family history

Great changes took place in Japan in the middle of the nineteenth century. The military dictatorship that had ruled the country for 650 years was overthrown and Emperor Meiji was installed as the head of the government. The feudal system was dismantled and Japan began to develop into a modern nation state. Led by the Emperor, the aristocrats and intellectuals began a lively debate about the future of the country.

At that time, my great-grandfather, Tanakaminamoto no Sukeyoshi, was also ready for a change. He was tired of the endless factional infighting of the aristocracy and wanted to rid himself of the onerous duties his position demanded.

When the Emperor decided to move the Imperial Capital from Kyoto, where it had been for over a millennium, to Tokyo, he saw his chance. My family's roots ran deep in their home soil, and they didn't want to leave Kyoto. As head of the family, my great-grandfather made the momentous decision to give back his title and join the ranks of the commoners.

Emperor Meiji pressed him to remain in the peerage but he proudly declared that he was a man of the people. The Emperor insisted that he at least retain his name, which he agreed to do. In daily life the family now uses the shortened form of Tanaka.

Though noble in sentiment, my great-grandfather's decision was disastrous for the family's finances. Giving up his title, of course, meant forfeiting the property that went along with it. The family's estates had covered a vast area of north-eastern Kyoto, from Tanaka Shrine in the south to Ichijoji Temple in the north, an area thousands of acres in size.

My great-grandfather and his descendants never recovered from the loss. They were unable to gain a foothold in the modern economy that was propelling the country, and languished in genteel poverty, living off their savings and thriving on their outmoded sense of inherent superiority.

From *The Geisha of Gion*, by Mineko Iwasaki (2003)

1. Rewrite the following quotations in your own words (given the context of the passage).

   a. "The military dictatorship that had ruled the country for 650 years was overthrown" (lines 2–4)

   ....

   ....

   b. "The feudal system was dismantled" (lines 5–6)

   ....

   ....

   c. "the endless factional infighting of the aristocracy" (lines 12–13)

   ....

   ....

   d. "the onerous duties his position demanded" (line 14)

   ....

   ....

   e. a "momentous decision" (line 21)

   ....

   ....

   f. "forfeiting the property" (line 32)

   ....

   ....

   g. "genteel poverty" (lines 40–1)

   ....

   ....

Now read the next passage in which Mineko Iwasaki explains something of her mother's family history and describes how her parents met. Then answer the question that follows.

Family history

My mother Chie is a member of the Akamatsu family. In olden times, they were legendary pirates who buccaneered the trade routes around the Inland Sea and out towards Korea and China, amassing a fortune in ill-gotten gains that they managed to transform into legitimate wealth by the time my mother came along. The Akamatsu family never served any *Daimyo* (military governor), but themselves had the power and property to govern Western Japan. The family was awarded the name Akamatsu by Emperor Gotoba (1180–1239).

While adventuring in 'foreign commodities' the family gained much knowledge about medicinal herbs and their preparation. They studied the art of healing and eventually rose to become house physicians to the Ikeda clan, the feudal barons of Okayama. My mother inherited these skills from her ancestors and passed her knowledge on to my father.

My parents were both artists. My father graduated from art school and became a professional painter of textiles for high quality kimono and an appraiser of fine porcelain.

My mother loved kimono. One day, while visiting a kimono shop, she happened to run into my father, who fell in love with her on the spot. He pursued her quite relentlessly. Their class differences were such that my mother felt a relationship was impossible. [...]

At the time my father was very successful and making a lot of money. His creations attracted the highest prices and he was bringing home a good income every month. But he was giving most of this to his parents, who had little other source of funds. My grandparents lived with their extended family in an enormous home in the Tanaka section of town that was manned by a large staff of servants. By the 1930s the family had gone through most of its savings. Some of the men had tried their hand at civil servant work, but nobody was able to hold on to a job for very long. They simply had no tradition of working for a living. My father was supporting the entire household.

So, even though my father wasn't the oldest son, my grandparents insisted that he and my mother live with them when they got married. Basically, they needed the money.

It was not a happy situation. My grandmother, whose name was Tamiko, was an overbearingly flamboyant character, both autocratic and short-tempered, the exact opposite of my gentle, docile mother. My mother was the one who had been raised like a princess, but my grandmother treated her just like a servant. She was abusive to her from the start and berated her constantly for her common background. There were some notorious criminals within the Akamatsu lineage and my grandmother acted as if my mother was polluted. She didn't think the young woman was nearly good enough for her son.

Grandmother Tamiko's hobby was fencing, and she was a master at wielding the *naginata*, or Japanese halberd. My mother's docility drove the older woman crazy and she started to taunt her by threatening her openly with the curved lance of her weapon. She'd even chase her around the house! It was bizarre and frightening. On one occasion, my grandmother went too far. She repeatedly slashed through my mother's *obi* (kimono sash), severing it from her body. That was the final straw.

From *The Geisha of Gion*, by Mineko Iwasaki (2003)

> **Appraiser:** a valuer, who judges the quality of something and may set its price.

2. Imagine you are either Mineko's mother or her father. Write an entry in your diary or journal for what happened on the day Grandmother Tamiko slashed through Chie's kimono sash with her sword. Include the following:

- what happened
- why Grandmother Tamiko was using a sword
- why Grandmother Tamiko bullied Chie
- what you think about Grandmother Tamiko's behaviour.

Write between 200 and 300 words.

Reminder

In this type of empathic question you are being asked to analyse, evaluate and develop material from the text. When a question starts with "You are…" or "Imagine you are…", re-read the passage from that person's point of view and then express what that person thinks, feels and/or imagines.

....

....

....

....

....

....

....

....

....

....

....

....

....

....

....

....

....

....

....

....

....

....

Using English: spot the mistakes!

In each of the sentences below there are two words in brackets. One is grammatically correct, the other may be something we say but is technically incorrect in this context. Choose the correct word(s) for these sentences.

a. After he had (run / ran) about a kilometer, he (sank / sunk) to his knees with exhaustion.

b. Cloth is (wove / woven) from a type of wool that has (grown / grew) on local sheep.

c. The timid deer was (drove / driven) into a narrow valley where it was (slew / slain) by a tiger.

d. A tree had (fell / fallen) during a storm; its branches lay (broke / broken) all around it.

e. The sketch had been (drew / drawn) by a famous painter whose name was (wrote / written) at the bottom of the picture.

f. I was (sat / sitting) in front of the television when I realised there was someone (stood / standing) behind me.

g. I (can / can't) hardly believe that you kept this secret to yourself!

h. We (can not / cannot) come to (yours / your house) tomorrow because we need to study for our maths exam on Tuesday.

i. The team usually wins but (its / it's) success is never guaranteed.

j. We knew it (was / were) wrong, but we laughed (a lot / alot) anyway.

Using a dictionary or thesaurus

Read the passage below, then answer the questions that follow.

In the late 16th and early 17th centuries, people from the British Isles were taking their already hybrid language to the New World and other lands across the sea, and expanding their vocabulary to suit new experiences. However, something else was happening to the words in the English language within the British Isles. The invention of printing and the immediate popularity of printed books meant the different forms of English spoken in the British Isles needed to be standardised. As books became cheaper and more people learned to read, spelling and grammar became more (but not entirely) fixed, and the dialect of London, where most publishing houses were set up, became Standard English.

The first English dictionary was published in 1604. It was called *A Table Alphabeticall* and was written by a schoolteacher named Robert Cawdray. Then came a series of dictionaries that explained, in a simplified form, strange and difficult words. For example, the *New World of English Words* by Edward Phillips was published in 1658 and dealt with difficult and technical terms mostly taken from earlier dictionaries.

The meaning of the word *thesaurus* is from the Greek *thēsauros* for storehouse or treasure. The original sense of a thesaurus as a dictionary or encyclopaedia of words was narrowed down to being a list of selected words, concepts and synonyms by the publication of Roget's *Thesaurus of English Words and Phrases* in 1852. Roget's classification system took nearly 50 years to perfect and his thesaurus was not published until he was 73 years old. Only 1000 copies of the first edition were printed. The original structure has changed little since 1852, although it now includes many scientific and technological words. Today, Roget's *Thesaurus of English Words and Phrases* is one of the most used reference books in the world.

There are now two main kinds of thesaurus: a Roget-type with a category system and an A-to-Z thesaurus that looks more like a dictionary. If you are using a Roget-type thesaurus, become familiar with the way words are organised. To find a word, you need to go to the index first. The index will tell you which words are nouns, verbs and adjectives and give you a number. You then look for that number in the main body of the thesaurus.

It is a good idea to look at alternative words to use in your writing and not limit yourself to the ones you think you know. However, take care not to use an interesting new word that doesn't fit the context of your sentence. An A-to-Z thesaurus will help you because it gives you definitions, but you still need to take care to use an appropriate word for the context.

Hybrid: something created by combining different elements, species or varieties.

1. Look at these alternatives for the verb *speak*.

inform	mention	tell	say	utter	mutter
pronounce	blurt out	declare	divulge	chatter	gossip

   a. Which of the verbs in the box fits in this sentence?

   He planned to speak to her the minute he got home; he would .... her the good news immediately.

   b. Is there a synonym below that you could use instead? If not, why not?

inform	intimate	apprise	acquaint
instruct	mention	state	reveal

2. Write an exemple sentence to show the meaning of each of the following verbs and phrasal verbs. They can all be used to replace *to see* or *to look at*.

   a. glance ....

   ....

   b. catch a glimpse of ....

   ....

   c. peer ....

   ....

   d. gaze ....

   ....

   e. observe ....

   ....

   f. peep ....

   ....

   g. distinguish ....

   ....

   h. catch sight of ....

   ....

   i. detect ....

   ....

   j. locate ....

   ....

3. The English language has a rich and wide vocabulary because it uses words from different origins. In choosing verbs, for example, we can say we *listened* to the radio and *heard* the news or we *watched* a football match and *saw* the winning goal.

Read the following passage about how we communicate and how people respond when we speak to them. Choose the appropriate verb from the box to fill each gap, using the correct tense (past/present). You can use the same verb more than once. Two examples have been done for you.

to ask	to speak	to inform	to tell	to request	to respond	to answer
to talk	to discuss	to chat	to reply			

Dutch is **(a)** spoken as the native language throughout the Netherlands, but many people also **(b)** speak English and other languages. The Dutch seem to have a natural ability for foreign tongues. Unfortunately I don't, and I certainly can't **(c)** .... a word of Dutch. When my train stopped in the Hague I had to **(d)** .... a porter at the station if he could tell me the way to the main shopping street in English. He **(e)** .... in English, but he **(f)** .... with such a curious intonation I didn't understand much of what he **(g)** .... I tried again in my bad school French, but he obviously couldn't understand what I was **(h)** .... so I looked around for someone else to **(i)** .... and found a policeman who **(j)** .... excellent English and seemed pleased to have an opportunity to **(k)** .... to someone. We **(l)** .... about this and that for some minutes. However, by the time I had managed to get away from the station (and the policeman) I had forgotten what I had been **(m)** .... I did eventually find the main shopping street, but to **(n)** .... the truth, I'm not sure how I got there.

Using English: splitting infinitives

The infinitive is usually two words as in *to read* or *to write*, but we sometimes contract these two words to one. For example:

- *I helped her **pack** her bag.* (I helped her **to pack** her bag.)

You may have heard of the grammatical offence of splitting the infinitive.

- *I helped her **to** <u>quickly</u> **pack** her bag.* ✗
- *I helped her **to pack** her bag <u>quickly</u>.* ✔

Splitting the infinitive means separating the two words of an infinitive (*to* + verb) by putting an adverb or other words between them. For example:

- *I can't claim **to** <u>completely and honestly</u> **understand** this explanation.* ✗

We often split infinitives when we are speaking, but it is incorrect and looks clumsy in writing so it should be avoided.

Identify the split infinitives in these sentences and rewrite each sentence correctly.

a. Ask Mrs Adams to briefly explain what she wants us to do for homework.

....

b. Do you promise to obediently and loyally follow your leader?

....

c. He tried to eloquently express his true emotions, but she laughed at him.

....

d. I am writing to humbly apologise for hurting your feelings.

....

e. Try to clearly and accurately describe what you see.

....

Using English: sinister words

Here is part of a project on the way the English language uses words related to left-handedness by a student named Jamie, who is the heroine of the novel *Left Out* by Jean Gill (2017).

Left-handers unite!

The English language is prejudiced against left-handers. The word 'left' is from the Saxon word 'lyft', which had two meanings: 'left' and 'useless'.

It is not all left to make someone else feel inferior – ban these words!

Word	Meaning	
maladroit	clumsy	(from the French for 'bad on the right')
gauche	clumsy	(from the French for 'left')
sinister	wicked	(from the Latin for 'left')
awkward	clumsy	(from the Middle English 'awke' meaning 'from the left')
gawky	unco-ordinated	(meaning 'from the left')
adroit	deft	(clever with hands from the French for 'right')
dexterous	good with hands	(from the Latin for 'right')
ambidextrous	good with both hands	(from the Latin for having two right hands)
right	straight, correct, not left	(from the Latin for straight, right (side))
righteous	good	
to have two left feet	to be clumsy	

IS IT ANY WONDER WE LEFT-HANDERS FEEL CLUMSY?!!

What did the Romans ever do for us?

The Romans invented the right-handed handshake as a way of showing you were not carrying a weapon… but if you were left-handed, you could shake hands right-handed AND stab someone with the dagger in your left hand – SINISTER!

The Romans gave us our alphabet, which reads from left to right –

COULD THAT BE WHY MORE LEFT-HANDERS ARE DYSLEXIC?

?dednah-tfel uoy erA   ?ylisae siht daer uoy naC

?ylisae erom siht daer uoy naC   .gnitirwdnah tfel-ot-thgir ni seiraid sih etorw icniVad odranoeL

From *Left Out*, by Jean Gill (2017)

Using Jamie's project to help you, find the answers to the clues below in the word search. Some of the words go from left to right, but a few are more tricky.

a	e	q	t	n	i	p	h	a	s	f	b
w	m	a	l	a	d	r	o	i	t	r	g
k	p	b	y	c	z	b	m	k	u	f	a
w	m	s	i	n	i	s	t	e	r	h	u
a	t	n	u	d	o	i	s	v	m	k	c
r	i	g	h	t	e	o	u	s	o	e	h
d	w	t	k	m	v	x	w	z	o	p	e
o	a	a	d	r	z	i	t	e	g	n	k
h	p	r	g	j	e	o	p	r	n	r	t
t	w	m	o	d	t	j	a	s	o	a	i
k	a	r	d	e	x	t	e	r	o	u	s
m	y	a	k	b	e	i	d	m	j	o	s

Clues

- clumsy 1
- clumsy 2
- clumsy 3
- deft
- good
- good with both hands
- good with hands
- wicked

Practising reading comprehension

Read this passage and answer the questions that follow on a separate sheet of paper.

The Phoenix

Lord Strawberry, a nobleman, collected birds. He had the finest aviary in Europe, so large that eagles did not find it uncomfortable, so well laid out that both humming birds and snow-buntings had a climate that suited them perfectly. But for many years the finest set of apartments remained empty, with just a label saying: "PHOENIX. Habitat: Arabia."

Many authorities on bird life had assured Lord Strawberry that the phoenix is a fabulous bird, or that the breed was long extinct. Lord Strawberry was unconvinced: his family had always believed in phoenixes. At intervals he received from his agents (together with statements of their expenses) birds which they declared were the phoenix but which turned out to be orioles, macaws, turkey buzzards dyed orange, etc., or stuffed cross-breeds, ingeniously assembled from various plumages. Finally Lord Strawberry went himself to Arabia, where, after some months, he found a phoenix, won its confidence, caught it, and brought it home in perfect condition.

It was a remarkably fine phoenix, with a charming character – affable to the other birds in the aviary and much attached to Lord Strawberry. On its arrival in England it made a greatest stir among ornithologists, journalists, poets, and milliners, and was constantly visited. But it was not puffed by these attentions, and when it was no longer in the news, and the visits fell off, it showed no pique or rancour. It ate well, and seemed perfectly contented.

It costs a great deal of money to keep up an aviary. When Lord Strawberry died he died penniless. The aviary came on the market. In normal times the rarer birds, and certainly the phoenix, would have been bid for by the trustees of Europe's great zoological societies, or by private persons in the U.S.A.; but as it happened Lord Strawberry died just after a world war, when

5

10

15

20

25

30

35

both money and bird-seed were hard to come by 40
(indeed the cost of bird-seed was one of the things
which had ruined Lord Strawberry). The London
Times urged in a leader that the phoenix be bought
for the London Zoo, saying that a nation of bird-
lovers had a moral right to own such a rarity; 45
and a fund, called the Strawberry Phoenix Fund,
was opened. Students, naturalists, and school-
children contributed according to their means; but
their means were small, and there were no large
donations. So Lord Strawberry's executors (who 50
had the death duties to consider) closed with the
higher offer of Mr. Tancred Poldero, owner and
proprietor of Poldero's Wizard Wonderworld.

For quite a while Mr. Poldero considered his
phoenix a bargain. It was a civil and obliging bird, 55
and adapted itself readily to its new surroundings.
It did not cost much to feed, it did not mind
children; and though it had no tricks, Mr. Poldero
supposed it would soon pick up some. The
publicity of the Strawberry Phoenix Fund was now 60
most helpful. Almost every contributor now saved
up another half-crown in order to see the phoenix.
Others, who had not contributed to the fund, even
paid double to look at it on the five-shilling days.

But then business slackened. The phoenix 65
was as handsome as ever, and amiable; but, as
Mr. Poldero said, it hadn't got Udge. Even at
popular prices the phoenix was not really popular.
It was too quiet, too classical. So people went
instead to watch the antics of the baboons, or to 70
admire the crocodile who had eaten the woman.

One day Mr. Poldero said to his manager,
Mr. Ramkin:

"How long since any fool paid to look at the
phoenix?" 75

"Matter of three weeks," replied Mr. Ramkin.

"Eating his head off," said Mr. Poldero. "Let
alone the insurance. Seven shillings a week it
costs me to insure the Archbishop of Canterbury."

"The public don't like him. He's too quiet for 80
them, that's the trouble. Won't mate nor nothing.
And I've tried him with no end of pretty pollies,
ospreys, and Cochin-Chinas, and the Lord knows
what. But he won't look at them."

"Wonder if we could swap him for a livelier 85
one," said Mr. Poldero.

"Impossible. There's only one of him at a time."

"Go on!"

"I mean it. Haven't you ever read what it says
on the label?" 90

They went to the phoenix's cage. It flapped its
wings politely, but they paid no attention. They read:

"PANSY. *Phoenix phoenixissima formossisima
arabiana*. This rare and fabulous bird is unique.
The World's Old Bachelor. Has no mate and 95
doesn't want one. When old, sets fire to itself
and emerges miraculously reborn. Specially
imported from the East."

"I've got an idea," said Mr. Poldero. "How old
do you suppose that bird is?" 100

"Looks in its prime to me," said Mr. Ramkin.

"Suppose," continued Mr. Poldero, "we could
somehow get him alight? We'd advertise it
beforehand, of course, work up interest. Then
we'd have a new bird, and a bird with some 105
romance about it, a bird with a life story.
We could sell a bird like that."

Mr. Ramkin nodded.

"I've read about it in a book," he said. "You've
got to give them scented woods and what not, 110
and they build a nest and sit down on it and
catch fire spontaneous. But they won't do it till
they're old. That's the snag."

"Leave that to me," said Mr. Poldero. "You get
those scented woods, and I'll do the ageing." 115

It was not easy to age the phoenix.
Its allowance of food was halved, and halved
again, but though it grew thinner its eyes were
undimmed and its plumage glossy as ever. The
heating was turned off; but it puffed out its 120
feathers against the cold, and seemed none the
worse. Other birds were put into its cage, birds of
a peevish and quarrelsome nature. They pecked
and chivvied it; but the phoenix was so civil and
amiable that after a day or two they lost their 125
animosity. Then Mr. Poldero tried alley cats.
These could not be won by manners, but the

phoenix darted above their heads and flapped its golden wings in their faces, and daunted them.

Mr. Poldero turned to a book on Arabia, and read that the climate was dry. "Aha!" said he. The phoenix was moved to a small cage that had a sprinkler in the ceiling. Every night the sprinkler was turned on. The phoenix began to cough. Mr. Poldero had another good idea. Daily he stationed himself in front of the cage to jeer at the bird and abuse it. 130 135

When spring was come, Mr. Poldero felt justified in beginning a publicity campaign about the ageing phoenix. The old public favourite, he said, was nearing its end. Meanwhile he tested the bird's reactions every few days by putting a few tufts of foul-smelling straw and some strands of rusty barbed wire into the cage, to see if it were interested in nesting yet. One day the phoenix began turning over the straw. Mr. Poldero signed a contract for the film rights. At last the hour seemed ripe. It was a fine Saturday evening in May. For some weeks the public interest in the ageing phoenix had been working up, and the admission charge had risen to five shillings. The enclosure was thronged. The lights and the cameras were trained on the cage, and a loud-speaker proclaimed to the audience the rarity of what was about to take place. 140 145 150 155

"The phoenix," said the loud-speaker, "is the aristocrat of bird-life. Only the rarest and most expensive specimens of oriental wood, drenched in exotic perfumes, will tempt him to construct his strange love-nest." 160

Now a neat assortment of twigs and shavings, strongly scented, was shoved into the cage.

"The phoenix," the loud-speaker continued, "is as capricious as Cleopatra, as luxurious as la du Barry, as heady as a strain of wild gypsy music. All the fantastic pomp and passion of the ancient East, its languorous magic, its subtle cruelties . . ." 165

"Lawks!" cried a woman in the crowd. "He's at it!"

A quiver stirred the dulled plumage. The phoenix turned its head from side to side. It descended, staggering, from its perch. Then wearily it began to pull about the twigs and shavings. 170

The cameras clicked, the lights blazed full on the cage. Rushing to the loud-speaker Mr. Poldero exclaimed: 175

"Ladies and gentlemen, this is the thrilling moment the world has breathlessly awaited. The legend of centuries is materializing before our modern eyes. The phoenix…" 180

The phoenix settled on its pyre and appeared to fall asleep.

The film director said:

"Well, if it doesn't evaluate more than this, mark instructional." 185

At that moment the phoenix and the pyre burst into flames. The flames streamed upwards, leaped out on every side. In a minute or two everything was burned to ashes, and some thousand people, including Mr. Poldero, perished in the blaze. 190

From *The Cat's Cradle Book*, by Silvia Townsend Warner (1960)

Milliners people who make women's hats.

Leader leading article in a newspaper.

Half-crown a coin worth two shillings and sixpence in old British money (a considerable amount in those days).

Archbishop of Canterbury Poldero is referring to the phoenix and its quiet respectability.

1. Answer the following questions in full sentences.

   a. Give one reason why Lord Strawberry wanted the phoenix.
      (1 mark)

   b. Describe the conditions in Lord Strawberry's aviary. (1 mark)

   c. Give one reason why Poldero acquires the phoenix. (1 mark)

   d. Describe what Poldero does with the phoenix to start with.
      (1 mark)

   e. Explain what Poldero means by "(the phoenix) hadn't got Udge"
      (line 69). (2 marks)

   f. In your opinion, why did people lose interest in the phoenix and go
      to see the crocodile instead? (2 marks)

   g. Explain why Poldero decides to 'age' the phoenix. (2 marks)

   h. Describe how Poldero encourages the phoenix to die. (3 marks)

   i. Explain when and why Poldero begins a publicity campaign.
      (2 marks)

   j. Describe what happened to the people who came to see the
      phoenix burst into flames. (2 marks)

   k. Re-read the last paragraph (starting with "At that moment...").
      Give your thoughts on why the author ended her story this way.
      (3 marks)

2. Re-read the different ways the phoenix is described at the beginning
   and end of the story. Examine:

   a. what the narrator says about the bird when it is acquired for
      Poldero's Wizard Wonderland

   b. what the loud-speaker says about the phoenix when the press and
      public come to see it die.

   Select words and phrases from these descriptions to show how the
   writer makes the reader feel sorry for the bird. (5 marks)

   (25 marks)

Reading comprehension

Read the following article about a hobo in North America and answer the questions that follow.

Another sort of life: A hobo in the USA

"Hobo" is the name given to a group of people, mostly men, who spend their days travelling across the USA hitching free rides on freight trains. One of these men, Jack Kotwinsky, turned his back on ordinary life, "getting and spending", 5 and chose to live the life of a hobo. He was known to everyone as Hippy John. Unlike many others who have chosen to drop out of consumer society, once he'd discovered the freedom of the road he never returned to mainstream American life. 10

When Hippy John was young and fit he'd run alongside slow-moving trains, grab onto a ladder at the side of a boxcar then swing himself up to safety. Gradually, age caught up with him, being slower and less agile he began boarding trains 15 in rail yards between journeys. Sometimes he was even helped by friendly security guards, who knew Hippy John meant no harm. For a period of twenty years he travelled the tracks that cross the United States from ocean to ocean. He kept 20 few possessions with him – only food and maps. His favourite routes, he said, were in the northern states, where he'd lie under the stars in open boxcars on warm nights while his train climbed mountain passes so narrow he could reach out 25 and touch the rocks either side.

But Hippy John's life was lonely. Sometimes, to relieve this loneliness, he would take trips with other hobos. These men shared food and drink, occasionally they told each other where they'd 30 been, but other than that they were united only by a shared sense of freedom. These hobos developed a special mutual respect born out of their love of being "away from it all". It was never a perfect life, but Hippy John wanted no other. 35

There are still many young and not-so-young men travelling the tracks across the USA. They are continuing a tradition dating back to the nineteenth century, when the British poet Wordsworth lamented how modern man was 40 becoming disconnected from the natural world. This was a hard time in North America, when southern farmers returning from the Civil War found their homes and towns in ruins. Homeless, with only the clothes on their backs, they took 45 the only jobs available – building the first railroad tracks. As they had once been farmers, they were called hoe-boys – then hobos. Many of them never settled again but instead spent their lives travelling the rail tracks they had built. 50

a. Explain where the word "hobo" comes from. (3 marks)

....

....

b. Explain what you understand by the phrase "mainstream American life". (3 marks)

....

....

c. Using your own words, briefly describe the hobo lifestyle. (3 marks)

....

....

d. Describe how Jack Kotwinsky boarded trains when he was young and in his more mature years. (2 marks)

....

....

e. Re-read the sentence "They are continuing a tradition… becoming disconnected from the natural world" (lines 37–41). Discuss what this suggests about why hobos choose to spend their lives travelling the tracks. (3 marks)

....

....

....

f. Re-read paragraphs 2 and 3. Choose three phrases used by the writer to suggest the pleasures Hippy John found in his hobo life and explain how they express this pleasure. (6 marks)

....

....

....

....

....

....

(20 marks)

Skimming, scanning and close reading

Think about how you read the article about American hobos and answer the questions below.

1. When and how did you skim the text?

....

....

....

....

2. Which type of questions could you answer by scanning the text?

....

....

....

....

3. Which type of questions required close reading of the text?

....

....

....

....

Using English: relative clauses

A **defining relative clause** gives essential information about the noun or noun phrase it modifies in order to identify exactly who or what is being referred to. Removing the information in this clause would result in the sentence having a different meaning or no meaning at all. For example:

The boy who stole my watch lives in my street.

If you remove the clause "who stole my watch", the sentence reads:

The boy lives in my street.

There are many boys living in your street. Which boy are you talking about?

1. Delete the defining relative clause from the following two sentences.

   a. The hotel that we stayed in on our school trip to London was very big.

   b. The guide who showed us round the Tower of London was very funny.

As you can see, the phrase "that we stayed in on our school trip to London" tells you which hotel is being referred to. There are thousands of hotels in London, so it defines the exact hotel.

There may be many amusing tour guides in London, but the phrase "who showed us round the Tower of London" identifies that we are referring to the one working in the Tower of London.

Non-defining relative clauses provide additional information that is not essential to understanding the meaning of the sentence. For example:

My best friend Terry, who keeps white mice, lives next door to us.

"My best friend Terry lives next door to us" provides a valid piece of information. The fact that he keeps white mice is interesting, but not essential to understanding where Terry lives. The information between commas about the white mice is a non-defining relative clause.

2. Delete the non-defining relative clauses from these sentences.

   a. The book we're studying this term, which I've read before, is called *Lord of the Flies*.

   b. *Lord of the Flies* tells the story of a group of boys who crash land on an island, which is situated somewhere in the Pacific Ocean, and how they survive without adults.

   c. George Orwell, who lived in what used to be called Burma when he was young, is famous for writing *Animal Farm* and *1984*.

   d. *Animal Farm*, whose real hero is a carthorse called Boxer, is an allegory of the Russian Revolution.

   e. The character of Boxer, who is very hardworking, represents Russian labourers.

> **Reminder**
>
> • *Who*, *whom*, *whose* and *that* are used for defining people.
>
> • *Which*, *whose* and *that* are used for things.
>
> • Defining relative clauses do not need commas.

As you can see, the non-defining relative clauses add extra information that is useful or interesting but not essential to the sentence.

3. Decide whether each of the following sentences contains a defining or a non-defining relative clause. The first one has been done for you.

	Defining	Non-defining
a. Marianne, who always comes top in tests, is the only girl I know who plays a trumpet.		✔
b. Paula can't go on the trip because her twin brother Joey, whose name is really Joshua, has broken his leg and she's got to stay at home to help look after him.		
c. Money that had been stolen from our school safe was found in a classroom.		
d. Jack's mother, who can play the violin, makes delicious cakes for our school tuck shop.		
e. Jack's mother's violin, which she'll be playing at our school charity concert, is extremely valuable.		

4. Write a short paragraph of more than two sentences about a book you have read recently. Vary your sentences so they contain defining and non-defining relative clauses.

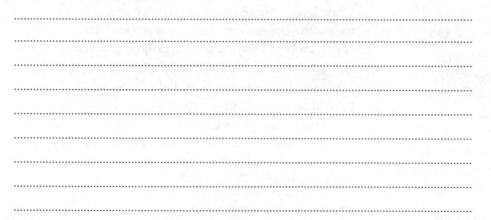

....

....

....

....

....

....

....

....

Directed writing

Read this blog post interview and do the Directed writing task that follows.

Rafael Selas, director of Anidan – our Wishmaker of the month!

By Carlota Nelson, The Toy blog (24 March 2014)

There are projects that are an open invitation for us to imagine a better world is possible. Projects that begin with a journey and a personal initiative. We're talking about projects like **Anidan**, an NGO that supports a home for 5 orphaned and abandoned children, a children's hospital and a system of micro-credits for women to start a small business to support their children. We had the honour of meeting **Rafael Selas**, founder and director of Anidan, someone 10 who many thought crazy or too naïve when he began to make his dream come true. Rafael started alone in 2002 and now has a small army of 80 workers and volunteers who help him with 250 children on the island of Lamu, in Kenya. 15 To us, this type of crazy makes us dream and keeps us inspired. That's why we made him our 'Wishmaker of the month'.

CN: Rafael, how did you start this project that now has representatives in Italy, Spain, 20 England and soon North America?

RS: It began when, contrary to everyone's opinion, I went to Lamu with the idea of renting a house and helping to support some of the children I had seen wandering among the 25 garbage or had malaria but didn't have the means to pay for medical attention. I realized that working in Africa was a tremendous task but a task that someone has to do. Large organizations or international organisms aren't enough. 30

CN: What projects has Anidan created?

RS: We have the orphanage and the hospital. Although we dedicate ourselves to the children and their future, we also need to take care of their families. We have also begun to offer micro- 35 credits to poor women who want to start small businesses. This way they can support their children and regain their dignity.

CN: How many people work at Anidan and how many children do you take care of? 40

RS: There are a total of 80 people who work at the hospital and the orphanage as cooks, cleaners, midwives, teachers, doctors and people in charge of the maintenance of the buildings and house. There are 250 children who come to school and 45 half of them sleep at the orphanage. We feed them, clothe them, take them to the doctor, and keep them in school, covering their basic needs. The hospital attends to 13,000 children a year and has 4,000 first aid camps. Everything is free of 50 charge for the children, including the medicines that they could not pay for.

CN: Would you like to share an anecdote?

RS: The majority of children who come to us are very young and carry a heavy burden on their 55 shoulders. A large part of our children are *borana girls*, who have escaped from wars and live in straw huts without water, electricity or a simple toilet. The borana girls belong to a tribe that doesn't believe women should progress. When 60 they get home they have to help with the heaviest chores and do not even have light under which to read or write. Many of these girls have secretly organized themselves to study and they are now at the top of their class. It's amazing to see how they 65 progress each year in their silent fight for their right to study.

CN: International scope?

RS: Our projects are located in Lamu, Kenya. Since 2011, we have a representative in Italy 70 and our ambassador in London is famous choreographer Wayne McGregor. This year we hope to launch Anidan United States.

CN: Who are *your* Wishmakers?

RS: Ever since I was young I have felt admiration 75
for Gandhi, Nelson Mandela and organizations
such as UNICEF, Red Cross and Greenpeace.
There are many other examples such as Vicente
Ferrer or Doctors without Borders. But today my
heroes are the people who help me every day. 80

CN: As a father and the director of Anidan, what advice would you give parents today?

RS: Make your children study, study, study.
It doesn't matter how bleak things appear, or
whether you are in Spain or Kenya, only by 85
studying will children and young people lead a
better life.

Read the interview with Rafael Selas carefully and write a short
informative article about his work with Anidan for your school magazine.

Write between 250 and 350 words. Use a separate sheet of paper if necessary.
Include:

- your opinion of what Anidan is doing in Lamu
- your views on whether your school could or should help
- ideas about how your school could help (if appropriate).

....
....
....
....
....
....
....
....
....
....
....
....
....
....
....
....
....
....
....
....
....

7 "Believe it or not"

Making words work: news reports

The purpose of a news report, whether it is online or in a printed newspaper, is to inform.

Newspaper reporters use short paragraphs and combine details as succinctly and effectively as possible. For example:

> Pensioner Tom Wood was trapped for ten hours in a tree during a 50km per-hour mini-hurricane while rescuing his neighbour's prize-winning cat.

A longer account of the event might read:

> Mr Thomas Wood, a retired railway engineer from north London with a serious heart condition, was forced to cling to the wildly swaying branch of a tree for ten hours last Thursday as strong winds gusting at a wind speed of 50 kph cut across southern England, destroying hedges and fences. His neighbour's cat, a prize-winning Persian Pink by the name of Little Missy Rose, had climbed…

1. Convert the words below into a one-sentence news report.

| tiger | escaped | private zoo |

| cat food | kitchen |

2. Read this blog post on fake news and answer the questions that follow.

Yellow journalism and fake news

By Jeffrey M. Berry, OUP blog (17 January 2017)

"Fake news" is in the news. As Jeffrey M. Berry, Professor of Political Science at Tufts University, says: "Anyone with a laptop and an Internet connection can be in the news business as citizen journalists." Quality and accuracy are not 5 important: what matters in fake news is that it's sensational and "clickable". The only requirement for creating fake news stories is an imagination. Berry goes on to say, "The technologically savvy can create bots which propel stories back and forth 10 among fake accounts, scoring hits and likes and pushing these articles to the top of trending news on Facebook and Google. Placed on a website, a story can be linked to an advertising service which generates a few pennies per click-through." 15

The current wave of fake news is nothing new. It has its origins in populist, sensational so-called "news" that focused on human interest stories, was often inaccurate, and obsessed with scandal. In the USA it was called "yellow journalism"; in 20 Britain it became known as "tabloid journalism". All newspapers need eye-catching headlines to grab their readers' interest and encourage sales, but tabloid or yellow journalism goes a step further: it's sensational. "Stories" are exaggerated 25 using "shock-horror!" phrasing to pique our curiosity. Like it or not, celebrity news sells, but the reader can always choose to believe it, or not.
. More on this at: http://blog.oup.com/2017/01/ economic-efficiency-fake-news 30

The writer of this blog post has used a variety of sentence types.

a. Count the sentences in paragraph 1. How many are there?

....

b. Identify two short, simple sentences (one verb) in paragraph 1. Give line references and explain why the writer has used them.

....

....

....

c. Identify two sentences in paragraph 1 where the writer has used a colon (:). Give line references and explain why the colon has been used in each.

....

....

....

d. Count the sentences in paragraph 2. How many are there?

....

e. Identify a sentence with a semi-colon (;). Give line references and explain how the semi-colon(s) are used.

....

....

....

Using English: adjectives and adjectival phrases

An adjective describes a noun. An adjectival phrase is a group of words that together describe a noun or pronoun in a sentence, thus functioning as an adjective.

A single adjective usually goes before the noun: *an **expensive** meal, a **huge** diamond*.

An adjectival phrase usually goes after the noun. For example:

- The meal was **expensive but delicious**.

- The diamond was **huge and obviously very expensive**.

As you can see, an adjectival phrase can contain words that are not adjectives, such as *and/but* (connectives) or *obviously* (adverb).

1. In each sentence identify the noun and the adjectival phrase. The first one has been done for you. Use red to underline the noun and yellow for the adjectival phrase.

    a. My holiday was wonderfully relaxing.

    b. The weather during the week was blissfully warm.

    c. We used the hotel swimming pool every day; it was heated and decorated with shells.

    d. My father caught a shark while he was fishing; it was quite small but had a huge mouth and needle-sharp teeth.

    | noun |

    | adjectival phrase |

2. Rewrite each sentence below to include extra information by using the words in brackets to make adjectival phrases. The first one has been done for you.

    a. The warrior wore a steel helmet. (shiny/lightweight)

    The warrior wore a helmet made of shiny lightweight steel.

    b. Everyone in the village was suffering from the effects of a drought. (devastating/year-long)

    ....

    ....

    c. They live in an old house. (dilapidated/16th-century/in need of repair)

    ....

    ....

    d. There is a Chinese vase on the table. (priceless/antique/finely decorated/Ming)

    ....

    ....

e. His action in the face of great danger resulted in a medal for bravery. (completely selfless/heroic)

....

....

3. Write three sentences containing adjectival phrases about one of the following:

- a concert
- a rescue
- a famous sportsman and/or sports event.

....

....

....

....

....

....

....

....

....

....

....

Exploring where poems come from

In the following two passages, two poets, James Reeves and Gillian Clarke, discuss how poems are formed. Read both passages and answer the questions that follow.

Passage A: Where do poems come from?

If a poem is not simply printed words on a page, or a notation for a series of spoken sounds, what is it? It is most helpful at this point, I think, to regard a poem as an event. At best, it is a magical event; and at worst it is only the feeble shadow [5] of an event, or, if you like, an event that doesn't happen. […] The poem doesn't simply describe or relate an event in the poet's mind; it is itself an event. It doesn't happen in the poet's mind or anywhere else until it is written down, or at any [10] rate composed in the poet's mind. Nobody can generalize about the way in which every poet writes. But I think it is true to say that usually some sort of disturbance happens in the poet's mind, and this takes shape as an event which can [15] be communicated to others through the medium of the written word. A thunderstorm is an event which takes place in the atmosphere as the result of an electrical disturbance. Electric charges build up in the atmosphere until their force is released [20] as lightning and thunder. A poem can occur when some sort of force or pressure builds up in the poet's mind and demands release in the form of a poetic event. Its appearance need not be sudden or explosive like a thunderclap; it may be slow and [25] gradual. Nor, I must add, does this describe all kinds of poem; but I think it describes many of the best.

Until the poem has formed itself in the poet's mind – and it is unlikely to form itself completely except during the actual process of composition – [30] the poet cannot be absolutely certain what he is going to write. Once it has been discharged from his mind, it takes its place in the series of events which go to make up the sum of all poetry. The reader to whose consciousness the new event is [35] communicated will not get from the poem exactly the experience that built up in the poet's mind before he wrote it. But if the poem is a good one – or, put it in another way, if the event is charged with magic – he and countless other readers can [40] receive from it a shock or surprise. This is the shock of having a new experience. The reader's experience has been permanently enlarged.

From *Understanding Poetry* by James Reeves (1967)

Passage B: Where do poems come from?

Where do poems come from? An architect sees an interior before he sees the building. Before a roof and walls there is space and light. That's how it feels when a poem is about to form: there is an idea, an image, a fuzzy line, a fizzing excitement, [5] but the words have yet to speak. Even if there are words it is somehow too dark to read them, though a phrase or a line may be legible already. But as soon as this unclear vision declares its presence one can be certain that the poem can be written. [10]

For me, the poem arrives in a coinciding moment of language and energy. Its subject is like a novelist's plot – merely an excuse to rummage in the mind for language. There are few plots and all writers share the same small store, using them [15] over and over again. When a poem is on the way it feels as though energy has been lying in wait for language. Or is it the other way about? And whence does that language come flooding, as strongly as any of the driving human passions, and as suddenly, [20] as mysteriously? The poem is begun in that moment of germination, though it must be unmade and made again in the cold light of the mind before it can be called a finished work of art. To have an *idea* for a poem is to have nothing at all. [25]

From *At the Source: A Writer's Year*, by Gillian Clarke (2008)

1. James Reeves likens a finished poem to an "event". Re-read lines 14–17 and explain in your own words what you think he means by "some sort of disturbance happens in the poet's mind, and this takes shape as an event".

....

....

....

2. In your own words explain what you think Reeves means by "The reader's experience has been permanently enlarged." (lines 42–3).

....

....

3. In your own words explain what you think Clarke means when she says the subject of a poem is an "excuse to rummage in the mind for language". (lines 13–14)

....

....

4. Clarke says a poem has to be "unmade and made again in the cold light of the mind before it can be called a finished work of art" (lines 22–4). Do you think all creative writing requires this process, or just poetry? Explain your thoughts.

....

....

....

5. Why, in your opinion, does Clarke say "To have an idea for a poem is to have nothing at all."? (lines 24–5)

....

....

6. The two poets talk about where poems come from in different ways. Is there any point on which they agree? Explain your thoughts.

....

....

....

....

....

Developing language appreciation: a poet's choice of words

White Sails of a Regatta

Early morning, warm at the north end
Of the Mar Menor, near a graveyard
Of small boats, colour of flaky bone.

Close to the broken hulls a few
Working boats are moored to life. 5
An old fish net yawns in the heat

On its drying-rack of spindly poles,
Its cross-struts parallel to the sea's surface
Are like grave markers against the sun.

I feel this is a movie scene not moving. 10
A seascape in still-life close-up.
On another old rack three nets drape

Like mourning shawls from its shoulder,
Weather, salt and water tatter it.
Light flickers fractals through the mesh. 15

Above flaked broken bodies of boats
Terns mock the air in stabbing flights
Mugging fish from one beak after another.

I sit on the beach taking it all in.
To my left an old man in orange waders 20
Untangles his worn net, mesh by mesh.

In a break for his fingers he tells me it has rotted
For years. He wonders if it's worth the trouble.
But adds that it gets him out of the house,

Out of his wife's hair as she prepares 25
    Sunday lunch.
We watch a sleek modern canoe pass silently
As the light wind drops to nothing.

Some metres offshore the Mar Menor glares.
Fills our eyes with painful light. The boats are
our still life. Like backlit graveyard furniture. 30

Under the surface some other world is pulling
Sunlight down to its own spectrum of shallows,
Fishermen, histories of catches. A few swallows

Sweep by, low over water, moving as fast
As their upside-down images allow. They go 35
Out beyond each boat dead or alive

To where the water is now blueing darkly
Below sails of a Regatta out of La Ribera.
Bright, triangular, against the Scoured Landscape.

Over there, southwest of here 40
Murcia airport's new control tower
Is merely a fuzzy thistlehead

While right in this foreground here
Reflections of an emerald green hull
Move silently like a pool of thick sap. 45

Green dips, then under sea-blue it seems.
A gust of wind scatters a bracelet of light loose,
Like bent ovals of water I've seen on lochs.

Here, each flaking boat, and each living hull
Rocks like sad seaweed in a slow, slow tide. 50
One peeling boat shrouded in its ruin of white

'La Virgen de Caridad', no longer sways.
She is laid here, falling apart, no rest in peace.
No bracelets of oval light now touch her.

Terns dive between her broken ribs. 55
The Regatta sails look like hooded mourners
Moving slowly in the heat-haze of Murcia.

By Neil mac Neil, from the New Writing Scotland 30
anthology *A Little Touch of Cliff in the Evening* (2012)

Regatta: boat or yacht races.

Mar Menor: a stretch of the Spanish Mediterranean coastline.

Waders: thigh-high waterproof boots.

Murcia: the Spanish province of Murcia, where the Mar Menor is located.

Lochs: Scottish lakes.

1. Explain how and why the poet uses the following words and phrases. You may quote from the poem to support your answers.

   a. "a graveyard / Of small boats" (lines 2/3)

   ....

   ....

   ....

   b. "a movie scene not moving" (line 10)

   ....

   ....

   ....

   c. "painful light" (line 29)

   ....

   ....

   ....

   d. "A gust of wind scatters a bracelet of light loose, / Like bent ovals of water" (lines 47/48).

   ....

   ....

   ....

2. Write a paragraph about how the words and images in "White Sails of a Regatta" convey a sense of time passing and/or sadness.

   ....

   ....

   ....

   ....

   ....

   ....

   ....

   ....

   ....

   ....

   ....

   ....

   ....

Reminder

Although there are no poems in the exams, reading poetry helps you to understand how words work and how words and phrases can be used to convey a tone or atmosphere.

8 World famous

Directed writing

Read the following articles posted on the Internet about the importance of taking safety seriously while climbing the mountain Mont Blanc in France. Then answer the question that follows.

Is Mont Blanc the World's most dangerous mountain?

28 January 2009

I remember standing on the small hill behind the Tete Rousse hut looking at the Gouter face of Mont Blanc, our proposed line of ascent. We were guiding a party of four clients and had guided on this [part of the mountain] many times in the past. This particular time was only two days after heavy snowfall and the face was seething with activity. Avalanches seemingly were coming down at random every 5 or 10 minutes. As we watched two climbers crossed the Grand Couloir. Halfway across, they started running as an avalanche came down the chute. They narrowly made it, escaping with their lives. A close call.

I informed my clients that, as they could see, the face was too dangerous to attempt in the current conditions. We should turn back and do something else. "Why?" came the reply. "They have just gone up," he said, pointing to the two lucky climbers. Another remarked, "My mate did it last year and said it was just a snow plod". They were not happy that I was not prepared to play Russian Roulette with their lives!

Stewart Green's "Guide to Climbing" says: Lots of people are killed and injured on [Mont Blanc] every year, and still they come in hordes to ascend to the roof of Europe. Why? Because the climbing is that good.

Some of the reasons are basically the same as those outlined in a 1902 article in the *New York Times*. The article cited a study of accidents from 1890 to 1901 by the Swiss Alpine Club, which found that 303 alpinists were killed in the Alps in that period. The study noted that the immediate causes of death included not employing a guide, climbing unknown routes from late fall to spring, foolhardy adventurousness, vanity, the spirit of emulation, want of experience and even absentmindedness!

[... The] 1,800ft Gouter Ridge on the approach to the Gouter hut, as loose and exposed to rock avalanches as it is, is still ascended in the main by helmetless climbers; these same climbers crossing and eventually recrossing the dangerous Grand Couloir whilst disdaining the use of basic safety equipment.

Thinking of ski-touring Mont Blanc? Think carefully!

Climbing and skiing Mont Blanc is exhilarating – but dangerous

It's the ultimate objective of European ski-mountaineers and backcountry skiers but believe me, this mountain must be taken seriously.

Yet what better way is there to spend summer than reaching the summit of Western Europe's highest peak then skiing down its fantastic 3000m off-piste descent?

During the ascent and descent you pass through spectacular glacial structures with deep crevasses and towering seracs – the scenery is simply breathtaking – but this is for experienced ski-tourers with a high level of fitness and no fear of adventure only! Warmer temperatures in recent years mean more crevasses have opened and you could be climbing some steep, exposed terrain.

The key to success on Mont Blanc is preparation plus a local, professional guide.

Safety is a priority. You also need to prepare for this trip with altitude training either in Chamonix or elsewhere in the Alps.

No matter how good you are on ski resort pistes, you'll need a course in ski-touring and ski-mountaineering. Basic requirements – you are:

- confident and safe doing kick turns on slopes of up to 35 degrees
- skilled with ice axe and crampons, and comfortable climbing steep terrain
- an advanced off-piste skier
- confident and safe skiing 40 degree slopes in all conditions (icy, crusty, powder)
- physically fit, ready to climb and ski for up to 8 hours (min) and repeat next day.

Reminder

Approach the question in the following way:

- Find relevant information and annotate the text.
- Think about what you have read and add your own thoughts.
- Read between the lines and develop both the information provided and what you have inferred from the writer's words.

You are preparing an off-piste summer ski-tour on Mont Blanc with a group of friends. This requires advanced climbing skills and ski techniques. Write a letter for your group about the trip. Include:

- the potential dangers of summer high-altitude climbing
- safety measures you consider necessary
- why being cautious should not spoil the trip.

Write between 250 and 350 words. Use a separate sheet of paper if necessary.

Reading comprehension and summary practice

The Bermuda Triangle is a fabled geographical area famous – or infamous – for the apparently inexplicable disappearance of ships, small boats and aircraft. The United States Coast Guard, however, does not accept that there is any specific hazard in the area. Read the two texts below and answer the questions that follow.

Text A: Gas leaks blamed for loss of boats and planes in the Bermuda Triangle

The disappearance of ships, boats and planes in the Bermuda Triangle has been blamed on UFOs, strange mists, even time travel. Some say there's a vortex that transports entire crews out of our universe. But scientists are now saying there is a more down-to-earth explanation. 5

The Bermuda Triangle covers 440,000 square miles of sea, from the North Atlantic Ocean to the Florida coast and on to Puerto Rico. Craters have been located in the Barents Sea measuring up to a half-mile wide and 150-feet deep, and filled 10 with methane. These craters could be why ships suddenly disappear.

Methane is believed to leak from deposits of natural gas below the sea bed; it then creates cavities which burst when the pressure gets 15 too high, scientists say. This would result in an explosion that could damage any boat, ship or plane passing at the time.

Russian scientist Igor Yeltsov, deputy head of 20 the Trofimuk Institute, says "There is a version that the Bermuda Triangle is a consequence of gas hydrates reactions. They start to actively decompose with methane ice turning into gas. It happens in an avalanche-like way, like a nuclear 25 reaction, producing huge amounts of gas." This causes sea water to heat up and the crater area is "likely to represent one of the largest hotspots for shallow marine methane release in the Arctic."

Whether this is actually happening in the 30 warmer waters off Florida is yet to be confirmed, but the fact remains, hundreds of boats and planes have been lost in the Bermuda Triangle since Christopher Columbus first recorded that his ship's compass stopped working when 35 he saw a fireball in the sky – off the coast of Bermuda.

Between four planes and 20 boats are reported missing without trace annually. One of the worst recorded losses was in 1945, when five 40 US Navy Avenger torpedo bombers flying from Fort Lauderdale, Florida, to Bimini Island never arrived. Radio calls from the crews stated their compasses had stopped working. Three rescue planes also disappeared. 45

Text B: What is the Bermuda Triangle?

[…] Some speculate that unknown and mysterious forces account for the unexplained disappearances, such as extraterrestrials capturing humans for study; the influence of the lost continent of Atlantis; vortices that 5 suck objects into other dimensions; and other whimsical ideas. Some explanations are more grounded in science, if not in evidence. These include oceanic flatulence (methane gas erupting from ocean sediments) and disruptions in 10 geomagnetic lines of flux.

Environmental considerations could explain many, if not most, of the disappearances. The majority of Atlantic tropical storms and hurricanes pass through the Bermuda Triangle, 15 and in the days prior to improved weather forecasting, these dangerous storms claimed many ships. Also, the Gulf Stream can cause rapid, sometimes violent, changes in weather. Additionally, the large number of islands in 20 the Caribbean Sea creates many areas of shallow water that can be treacherous to ship navigation. And there is some evidence to suggest that the Bermuda Triangle is a place where a "magnetic" compass sometimes   25 points towards "true" north, as opposed to "magnetic" north.

The U.S. Navy and U.S. Coast Guard contend that there are no supernatural explanations for disasters at sea. Their experience suggests   30 that the combined forces of nature and human fallibility outdo even the most incredulous science

fiction. They add that no official maps exist that delineate the boundaries of the Bermuda Triangle. The U. S. Board of Geographic Names does not   35 recognize the Bermuda Triangle as an official name and does not maintain an official file on the area.

The ocean has always been a mysterious place to humans, and when foul weather or poor navigation is involved, it can be a very deadly place. This is   40 true all over the world. There is no evidence that mysterious disappearances occur with any greater frequency in the Bermuda Triangle than in any other large, well-travelled area of the ocean.

1. Explain in your own words why the Bermuda Triangle is infamous.

....

....

....

2. Re-read Text A and Text B. Summarise why some people believe the Bermuda Triangle has a logical and/or scientific explanation and why others do not. Write no more than 120 words.

....

....

....

....

....

....

....

....

....

....

....

....

....

....

....

....

....

....

Using English: persuasive language

Here are two famous speeches made during the 19th century in the USA. Read them carefully and then look at how the speakers try to persuade their audiences to their way of thinking.

This first speech was made impromptu (without preparation or notes) by an ex-slave named Sojourner Truth at the Women's Convention in Akron, Ohio in 1851. When it was published in 1863 by Frances Gage it was given the title 'Ain't I a Woman?'

Sojourner Truth (1797–1883) was born in slavery but escaped with her infant daughter in 1826. Apart from giving this moving speech, she became famous for being the first black woman to ever win a court case against a white man.

Ain't I a woman?

Well, children, where there is so much racket there must be something out of kilter. I think that 'twixt the negroes of the South and the women at the North, all talking about rights, the white men will be in a fix pretty soon. But what's all this here 5 talking about?

That man over there says that women need to be helped into carriages, and lifted over ditches, and to have the best place everywhere. Nobody ever helps me into carriages, or over mud- 10 puddles, or gives me any best place! And ain't I a woman? Look at me! Look at my arm! I have ploughed and planted, and gathered into barns, and no man could head me! And ain't I a woman? I could work as much and eat as much as a 15 man – when I could get it – and bear the lash as well! And ain't I a woman? I have borne thirteen children, and seen most all sold off to slavery, and when I cried out with my mother's grief, none but Jesus heard me! And ain't I a woman? 20

Then they talk about this thing in the head; what's this they call it? [member of audience whispers, "intellect"] That's it, honey. What's that got to do with women's rights or negroes' rights? If my cup won't hold but a pint, and yours holds a 25 quart, wouldn't you be mean not to let me have my little half measure full?

Then that little man in black there, he says women can't have as much rights as men, 'cause Christ wasn't a woman! Where did your Christ 30 come from? Where did your Christ come from? From God and a woman! Man had nothing to do with Him.

If the first woman God ever made was strong enough to turn the world upside down all alone, 35 these women together ought to be able to turn it back, and get it right side up again! And now they is asking to do it, the men better let them.

Obliged to you for hearing me, and now old Sojourner ain't got nothing more to say. 40

The famous American president Abraham Lincoln gave this speech on the 9 November 1863 at the dedication of the Soldiers' National Cemetery at Gettysburg, the site of one of the bloodiest battles in the American Civil War. In this short speech Lincoln calls upon the principles of human equality and dignity contained in the Declaration of Independence and connects the sacrifices made on both sides fighting in the Civil War. He expresses the American desire for "a new birth of freedom" and the importance of preserving the self-governing Union that was created in 1776.

Lincoln was the second person to address the crowd that day: the first speaker was a famed orator named Edward Everett, who spoke for two hours. The following day Everett wrote to Lincoln saying, "Permit me also to express my great admiration of the thoughts expressed by you, with such eloquent simplicity and appropriateness, at the consecration of the Cemetery. I should be glad, if I could flatter myself that I came as near to the central idea of the occasion, in two hours, as you did in two minutes."

Gettysburg Address

Fourscore and seven years ago our fathers brought forth on this continent a new nation, conceived in liberty and dedicated to the proposition that all men are created equal.

Now we are engaged in a great civil war, 5 testing whether that nation or any nation so conceived and so dedicated can long endure. We are met on a great battlefield of that war. We have come to dedicate a portion of that field as a final resting-place for those who here gave their lives 10 that that nation might live. It is altogether fitting and proper that we should do this.

But, in a larger sense, we cannot dedicate, we cannot consecrate, we cannot hallow this ground. The brave men, living and dead, who struggled 15 here have consecrated it far above our poor power to add or detract. The world will little note nor long remember what we say here, but it can never forget what they did here. It is for us the living, rather, to be dedicated here to the unfinished 20 work which they who fought here have thus far so nobly advanced. It is rather for us to be here dedicated to the great task remaining before us that from these honored dead we take increased devotion to that cause for which they gave the last full 25 measure of devotion – that we here highly resolve that these dead shall not have died in vain, that this nation under God shall have a new birth of freedom, and that government of the people, by the people, for the people shall not perish from the earth. 30

Reminder

Rhetorical questions show the audience the situation so that the answer offered seems to be the only right thing to do.

Rule of three (tripling) gives three examples to reinforce a point, using powerful adjectives, so the audience remembers it.

Alliteration helps to make words memorable, e.g. **We will win this war!**

Hyperbole exaggerates the bad, accentuates the good so the audience can 'feel' that experience.

Including the audience (using e.g. *us*, *we*, *together*) addresses them directly, uniting them and making them feel they belong together with the speaker.

Destroying the opposition's argument in a polite and reasonable way works best.

Emotive language affects the way the audience feels, e.g. making them sad or sorry, offering them hope and making them want to take action.

Consecrate: to declare as sacred or holy.

Hallow: to consecrate or make holy.

Using the techniques in the Reminder box, answer the following questions. Quote from the speeches to support your views.

1. How does Sojourner Truth include her audience?

....

....

2. Why is this so significant in her speech?

....

....

3. How does Abraham Lincoln use the tripling technique?

....

....

4. How does Lincoln include his audience?

....

....

5. Why, in your opinion, is this important in Lincoln's speech?

....

....

6. Explain how and why Sojourner Truth uses the rhetorical question "Ain't I a woman?".

....

....

....

....

....

....

....

....

....

....

....

....

....

....

....

....

....

7. Sojourner Truth's impromtu speech was so important that it was written down and published. Select words and phrases from her speech and explain how they may have affected listeners at the time. Quote from the speech and explain the effects of her words.

....

....

....

....

8. The Gettysburg Address is still famous today. Select words and phrases from Lincoln's speech to explain how they may have affected listeners at the time. Quote from the speech and explain the effects of his words.

....

....

....

....

9. Using either Sojourner Truth's speech or Lincoln's address as a model, write a paragraph for a speech on something about which you feel strongly.

Aim to persuade your audience to your way of thinking as briefly and effectively as possible.

....

....

....

....

....

....

....

....

....

....

....

....

....

....

....

....

9 Endings

Practising reading skills

Read the following fiction passages and time how long it takes you to read each one. Then answer the reading comprehension questions that follow. Time how long it takes you to make notes and answer each question.

In this first passage you hear the voice of 11-year-old Laurie talking about his teacher, Miss Glennie. The school is in a fictional town in the north-east of England. As you read, underline words or phrases and make notes in the margin on how the author presents the scene from a child's point of view.

The narrator's voice

At last there has been something really good happening at my new school. We had a sort of a history lesson and Miss Glennie told us about boy chimney sweeps. She has got a book like the books in my father's study (only his are thicker 5 and the writing is much, much smaller) and I think books like that are about a hundred years old. She reads a bit out of this book and then we talk about it. She was reading today about the way of training a climbing boy, which is what 10 they used to call the sweeps' boys; how to wash their knees in salty water and scrub their knees with a hard brush every day, so no matter how much they scrape inside the chimney it will not hurt. It does at first, of course. In those days their 15 trousers went into rags quite quickly, so they cut themselves on the stones of the chimneys.

   When it was the time for the whole class to discuss this, I was the first one to ask things. Did they bleed a lot? How did the sweep find the boys 20 when they had finished? Did the boys die? Were they my size? Why did they climb if it hurt?

Miss Glennie said other people should have a chance to ask questions. Micka said he would have run away. 25

"But Michael," Miss Glennie said in her kind and soft voice, "these poor boys had no choice. For them, it was work or starve. Sometimes it was their own fathers who were the sweeps and they beat them to make them climb higher." 30

I asked again – Why did they climb if it hurt and their knees were bleeding like you said? Why didn't they come down again?

Miss Glennie opened her eyes wide.

"The sweeps would light a fire in the grate of 35 the chimney when the boys were up, to make them go faster. They would breathe the smoke and get scared of choking. So the boys would climb quickly to the top so they could breathe the fresh air. Sometimes the smoke made them too dizzy 40 to hold on any longer, and they let go and fell into the fire."

"Why didn't their mothers come and save them?" Lisa Carmichael asked that. What a stupid question to ask; such a girl question. All the other 45 girls looked as if they were going to be sick. Miss Glennie's voice got very sad and she said, "Very often they were orphans. They didn't have mothers."

Now, that is what I call a good lesson. If every day was like that I would be at school more often. 50 Unfortunately, then Miss Glennie made us do some writing about "I am a climbing boy (or girl, even though girls did not do it but at school we must always say girls can do anything boys can do, even if it is something cruel that hurts, like climbing 55 chimneys) and what are my feelings about chimney sweeping." This could have ruined a brilliant lesson, except I didn't do the writing, just a kind of a cartoon picture of a sweep lighting a huge fire with a most evil grin on his wicked face, 60 and in the next picture a little skinny boy climbing up and up, with a balloon coming out of his mouth saying, "Can't breathe, choking, cough cough." The boy looked like Micka. I showed it to him but he said my drawing was rubbish. Miss Glennie gave 65 me a green star for the picture (of course), but she put underneath; "Where is your writing, Laurie?". She is too soft. A real teacher would have torn up the picture and kept me in as a punishment.

From *Micka*, by Frances Kay (2010)

1. Using two examples from the passage to support your ideas, explain how the author presents this scene from Laurie's point of view.

....
....
....

> **Sweeps' boys**: until the late 19th century, the boys who climbed chimneys to clear the soot out for the men (sweeps) employed to clean chimneys.

2. The narrator, Laurie, asks the teacher why a boy continued to climb a chimney if it made his knees bleed. In your own words explain the teacher's response to this question.

....
....
....

3. One girl asks a question. Describe the narrator's reaction to her question in your own words.

....

....

....

4. Why, in your opinion, does Laurie not do the writing task as the teacher requested?

....

....

5. Miss Glennie gives Laurie a green star for his cartoon picture although it is not what she asked the class to do. Give one reason why she may have done this.

....

....

6. You are Miss Glennie. Your head teacher wants a short report on Laurie. Summarise Laurie's behaviour, attitude and class work in your lessons. Write no more than 120 words.

....

....

....

....

....

....

....

....

....

....

....

....

....

....

....

....

....

....

Now read two passages about a young girl living in France during the Second World War. In Passage A nine-year-old Boise wants to go to the cinema with her older brother Cassis and sister Reinette (Reine). She can only go if she can pay for her ticket. Boise hasn't got any money, but she knows where to find some. She prepares to raid Cassis' "Treasure Chest".

Passage A: Treasure Chest

At five in the morning the Loire is still and sumptuous with mist. The water is beautiful at that time of the day, cool and magically pale, the sandbanks rising like lost continents. The water smells of night, and here and there a spray of new 5
sunlight makes mica shadows on the surface. I took off my shoes and my dress and surveyed the water critically. It looked deceptively still.

The last of the Standing Stones, the Treasure Stone, was maybe thirty feet from the bank, and 10
the water at its base looked oddly silky at the surface, a sign that a strong current was at work. I could drown here, I told myself suddenly, and no one would even know where to look for me.

But I had no choice. Cassis had issued a 15
challenge. I had to pay my own way. How could I do that, with no pocket money of my own, without using the purse hidden in the Treasure Chest? Of course, there was a chance he might have removed it. If he had, I would risk stealing from my 20
mother's purse. But that I was reluctant to do. Not because stealing was especially wrong, but because of my mother's unusual memory for figures. She knew what she had to the last centime, and she would know at once what I had done. 25

No. It had to be the Treasure Chest.

Since Cassis and Reinette had finished school there had been few expeditions to the river. They had treasure of their own – *adult* treasure – to gloat over. The few coins in the purse amounted 30
to a couple of francs, no more. I was counting on Cassis' laziness, his conviction that no one but he would be able to reach the box tied to the pillar. I was sure the money was still there.

Carefully, I scrambled down the bank and 35
into the water. It was cold and river mud oozed between my toes. I waded out until the water was waist deep. I could feel the current now, like an impatient dog at the leash. God, it was already so strong! I put out a hand against the first pillar, 40
pushing away from it into the current, and took another step. I knew there was a drop just ahead, a point at which the still-shallow verge of the Loire sheared away into nothingness. Cassis, when he was making the trip, always pretended 45
to drown at this point, turning belly-up into the opaque water, struggling and screaming, with a mouthful of brown Loire spurting from between his lips. He always fooled Reine, however many times he did this, making her squeal in horror as 50
he sank beneath the surface.

I had no time for such an exhibition. I felt for the drop with my toes. There. Pushing against the riverbed, I propelled myself as far as I could with my first kick, keeping the Standing Stones 55
downriver to my right.

From *Five Quarters of the Orange*,
by Joanne Harris (2001)

1. Describe where the treasure chest is located.

....

....

2. Describe the contents of the chest.

....

....

3. Explain why Boise does not want to risk taking money from her mother's purse.

....

....

4. Give two examples from Passage A to show what Boise is doing is dangerous.

....

....

....

5. Why, in your opinion, does the author include the information that Cassis "always pretended to drown at this point, turning belly-up" in lines 45–6?

....

....

6. Explain why, from Boise's point of view, it is necessary to swim out to the treasure chest.

....

....

7. In your own words explain how and why the reader fears for Boise's safety.

....

....

....

....

Passage B: Treasure Chest

The water was warmer on the surface, and the drag of current not as strong. I swam steadily, in a smooth arc, from the first Standing Stone to the second. The stones were maybe twelve feet apart at their widest stretch, spread unevenly 5 from the bank. I could make five feet with a good strong kick against each pillar, aiming slightly upstream so the current would bring me back to the next pillar in time to begin again. Like a small boat tacking against a strong wind, I limped 10 towards the Treasure Stone, feeling the current grow stronger each time. I was gasping with cold. Then I was at the fourth pillar, making my final lunge towards my goal. As the current dragged me towards the Treasure Stone I overshot the 15 pillar, and there was a moment of sudden, sparkling terror as I began to move downstream into the main drag of the river, my arms and legs pinwheeling against the water. Panting, almost crying with panic, I managed to kick myself 20 within range of the stone, and grabbed the chain that secured the Treasure Chest to the pillar. It felt weedy and unpleasant in my hand, slimed with the brown ooze of the river, but I used it to manoeuvre myself around the pillar. 25

I clung there for a moment, letting my pounding heart quiet. Then, with my back wedged safely against the pillar, I hauled the Treasure Chest up and out of its muddy cradle. It was a difficult job. The box itself was not especially 30 heavy, but weighted with chain and tarpaulin as it was, it seemed a dead weight. Trembling with cold now, my teeth clattering, I struggled with the chain and finally felt something give. Kicking my

legs frantically to keep my position against the 35 pillar, I hauled at the box. I knew another moment of near panic as the mud-slimed tarpaulin caught at my feet, then my fingers were working at the rope which held the box. For an instant I was sure my numbed fingers would not be able to open the 40 tin, then the catch gave way and water rushed into the Treasure Chest. I swore. Still, there was the purse, an old brown leather thing Mother had discarded because of a faulty catch. I grabbed it and jammed it between my teeth for safety, then, 45 with a final effort, I slammed the box closed and let it sink, weighted by its chain, to the bottom again. The tarpaulin was lost, of course, the remaining treasure waterlogged, but that couldn't be helped. Cassis would have to find somewhere 50 drier to hide his cigarettes. I had the money, and that was all that mattered.

I swam back to the bank, missing the last two pillars and drifting 200 yards down towards the Angers road before I managed to steer myself out 55 of the current, which was now more like a dog than ever, a mad, brown dog with its leash twined crazily around my frozen legs. The whole episode, I guessed, had taken maybe ten minutes.

I forced myself to rest awhile, feeling the slight 60 warmth of the sun's first rays on my face, drying the mud of the Loire on my skin. I was trembling with cold and exhilaration. I counted the money in the purse; there was certainly enough for a cinema ticket and a glass of squash. 65

From *Five Quarters of the Orange*,
by Joanne Harris (2001)

Tarpaulin: a waterproof sheet material used to protect things from moisture.

1. Summarise how Boise finally obtains the money she needs to go to the cinema. Use your own words as far as possible.

Write no more than 120 words.

....

....

....

....

....

....

....

....

....

....

....

....

....

....

....

....

....

....

....

....

....

....

2. Re-read Passage A and Passage B. You are on the riverbank when Boise swims out to get her "treasure".

Write an entry for your journal giving your thoughts on what you saw the girl do.

Write between 200 and 300 words.

Use a separate sheet of paper if necessary.

....

....

....

....

....

10 Exam practice

Preparing for Paper 1

This text is a report from *The Guardian* newspaper about the impact of plastic bottles on the environment. Read the text carefully and then answer the summary question that follows.

A million bottles a minute

By Sandra Laville and Matthew Taylor, *The Guardian*
(28 June 2017)

A million plastic bottles are bought around the world every minute and the number will jump another 20% by 2021, creating an environmental crisis some campaigners predict will be as serious as climate change. The demand, [5] equivalent to about 20,000 bottles being bought every second, is driven by an apparently insatiable desire for bottled water and the spread of a western, "drinking on the go" culture to China and the Asia Pacific region. [10]

Most plastic bottles used for soft drinks and water are made from polyethylene terephthalate (Pet), which is highly recyclable. But as their use soars across the globe, efforts to collect and recycle the bottles to keep them from polluting the oceans [15] are failing to keep up. Instead most plastic bottles produced end up in landfill or in the ocean.

Between 5m and 13m tonnes of plastic leaks into the world's oceans each year to be ingested by sea birds, fish and other organisms, and by 2050 [20] the ocean will contain more plastic by weight than fish, according to research by the Ellen MacArthur Foundation.

Experts warn that some of it is already finding its way into the human food chain. [25]

Scientists at Ghent University in Belgium recently calculated people who eat seafood consume up to 11,000 tiny pieces of plastic every year.

Scientists have warned that plastic bottles [30] and other packaging are ruining some of the UK's most beautiful beaches and remote coastline, endangering wildlife from basking sharks to puffins.

China is responsible for most of the increase [35] in demand. "There is a desire for healthy living and there are ongoing concerns about the quality of tap water, which all contribute to the increase in bottle water use," said Rosemary Downey, an expert in plastic bottle production. 40

Plastic drinking bottles could be made out of 100% recycled plastic, known as RPet – but brands are hostile to using RPet because they want their products in shiny, clear plastic, according to Steve Morgan, of Recoup in the UK. 45

The industry is also resisting any taxes or charges to reduce demand for single-use plastic bottles – like the 5p charge on plastic bags that is credited with reducing plastic bag use by 80%. Louisa Casson, campaigner for Greenpeace, says: 50 "It's clear that the soft drinks industry needs to reduce its plastic footprint."

According to this text, what problems are caused by plastic drinking bottles and why is it difficult to solve these problems?

You must use continuous writing (not note form) and your own words as far as possible.

Write no more than 120 words. Up to 10 marks are available for the content of your answer and up to 5 marks for the quality of your writing.

....
....
....
....
....
....
....
....
....
....
....
....
....
....
....
....
....
....
....
....
....

Preparing for reading questions

Read the text below carefully and then answer the questions that follow.

Rescued

Alice is in India with her husband, whom she has just married, when a tsunami strikes. She has been swept away by the water and is rescued by a person she doesn't know.

Something cuffs itself to my wrists, hoisting me out of the water and giving me my air back. Rasps and rasps of it. I can't take it in properly – each breath a stammer. There's something sharp scraping across my belly. My shirt is rucking up. 5
I'm being dragged out of the sea.

"Help" is my first word, frail, half formed. I don't understand the reply I'm given. Tamil or Malayalam, maybe. It's a man's voice. There's a rough, rusting surface beneath me that feels 10
powdery and metallic on my fingers. It fits unevenly under my shoulders, the metal arching into sharp peaks and troughs. But we're floating. And that's all that counts.

The voice is shouting now but I still don't 15
understand. The salt water dissipates in stinging blinks; I begin to make out the man's shape. He's soaked to the skin, like me, in a checked lungi and plain shirt, hair wired with grey. His face, creased with years, is washed into blankness at the sight 20
of me and everything that's gone before us.

"Vana-kkam," I reply. One of the few words I know in Tamil. Good morning. I must sound ridiculous. He's smiling. At least that's something.

"Ongelal payse…" I don't catch the rest. And 25
even if I did, it would be useless.

"I don't understand. I'm so sorry."

He tips his head from left to right and back again. Then his hands rise and leap into action, eyes widening as he gestures towards the shore. 30
He mimics the wave coming in as he speaks, then knocks the metal underneath him with his knuckles, drawing out the shape of a square in the air with his two index fingers. He points to his chest and bangs the metal again, rattling out 35
his sentences so that I'm sure I wouldn't catch everything even if we did speak the same language.

"Your house? This is your house?" I watch him draw the shape in the air again and point down at the sheet of metal. 40

"House." He knocks on the metal for the third time. I force myself to sit up and look down at our makeshift raft. It is nothing more than a sheet of corrugated iron – a roof. Something catches his eye and he grabs me by the wrist, like he did 45
when he rescued me. He points to my ring, then down at the house and then back at the shore, face stiffening.

I catch only one word from what he is saying: Manaavi. James and I learnt it yesterday – our 50
wedding day. He said he preferred the sound of it to "wife". I meet his stare which is taut, unblinking. Raising my hand, I point to my ring and then to the shore, just as he did. "Kanavar," I whisper, "my husband." 55

I talk in English, telling him about James – and our wedding – how not even our parents know what we have done. How I don't know where he is – that I need to go and look for him. He speaks Tamil back to me, accompanying his 60
words, with broad, bold hand movements, which I watch, eager to interpret what he is saying. I try to discern the verbs and nouns from his tones, holding each sound in my head and attempting to dissect it. In the end, I have to let his sentences 65
go – they don't yield their logic easily and the words blur together. He turns away from me after a while, frustrated at not being understood. We resume our gaze at the sea.

Minutes pass like hours, hours like minutes. 70
Time dries in our throats. Flotillas of drinking
water appear on the horizon if I stare at it for too
long. The sun becomes what I want it to be – a
giant parasol cocooning me like night – instead of
what it is: unbearably bright and scorching. 75

And all the while we're floating, riding the roof
as if it were the saddle of a horse, never still.
        Night comes. And then day. Time gathers.
And gathers again. Waves bloat and expire.

From *The Sea Change*, by Joanna Rossiter (2013)

Lungi: a kind of sarong/clothing worn round the waist.

1. Identify a word or phrase from the text which suggests the same idea as the <u>words underlined</u>.

    a. Alice is able to <u>breathe</u> again. (1 mark)

    b. Alice is unable to <u>speak clearly</u>. (1 mark)

    c. The surface Alice is lying on is <u>not flat</u>. (1 mark)

    d. The man's face looks <u>old</u>. (1 mark)

2. Using your own words, explain what the writer means by each of the <u>words underlined</u>. (3 marks)

    He tips his head from left to right and back again. Then his hands
    rise and leap into action, eyes <u>widening</u> as he gestures towards the
    shore. He <u>mimics</u> the wave coming in as he speaks, then knocks
    the metal underneath him with his knuckles, drawing out the
    shape of a square in the air with his two index fingers. He points to
    his chest and bangs the metal again, <u>rattling</u> out his sentences so
    that I'm sure I wouldn't catch everything even if we did speak the
    same language.

    ....

    ....

    ....

3. Use **one** example from the text in question 2 to explain how the writer suggests the man's thoughts and feelings. (3 marks)

    ....

    ....

    ....

    ....

    ....

    ....

4. Re-read paragraphs 11 and 12: "I talk in English… never still."
   Paragraph 11 is about Alice and her rescuer trying to communicate
   with each other, while paragraph 12 is about their experience as they
   float on the water in the heat.

   Explain how the writer uses language to convey meaning and create
   effect in these paragraphs. Choose three examples of words or phrases
   from each paragraph to support your answer. Your choices should
   include the use of imagery.

   Write between 200 and 300 words. Up to 15 marks are available for
   the content of your answer.

....
....
....
....
....
....
....
....
....
....
....
....
....
....
....
....
....
....
....
....
....
....
....
....
....
....
....
....
....
....

Exam practice 10

5. You are the man who rescued Alice. You are interviewed about your experience. You tell the interviewer about:

- how you managed to pull the woman from the water and your first impressions of her
- how you tried to communicate with each other and what you learned about her
- the challenges you faced stranded on your makeshift raft in the heat and what you thought might happen to you.

Base what you write on what you have read in the text, but be careful to use your own words. Address each of the three bullet points.

Write between 250 and 350 words. Up to 15 marks are available for the content of your answer and up to 10 marks for the quality of your writing.

....
....
....
....
....
....
....
....
....
....
....
....
....
....
....
....
....
....
....
....
....
....
....
....

Preparing for Directed Writing and Composition

Read the following passages about English pantomimes and then answer the directed writing and composition questions that follow.

What a pantomime!

British pantomime is a traditional winter entertainment, a musical comedy with topical humour, popular celebrities and television stars. Modern pantomimes are still based on traditional fairy stories such as Cinderella, Aladdin, Dick Whittington, Snow White. Scriptwriters add contemporary references to politics, sport and television, and   5
provide plenty of opportunity for audiences to get involved in the action. Pantomimes are colourful, noisy, good fun and great family entertainment. In fact they're a must for any family.

British pantomime dates back to 15th- and 16th-century traditions of Comedia dell'arte in which there are stock characters   10
and stage conventions. In every pantomime there is:

- a principal boy played by a girl with long legs in a tight costume

- the pantomime dame, who's a man in women's clothes that no woman would ever wear   15

- a chorus figure, the principal boy's brother or friend, who speaks directly to the audience

- an animal, usually a cow, played by two actors in one costume

- a villain, who is hissed at by the audience

- lots of audience participation that includes shouting, "Look   20
behind you!" and the traditional "Oh yes it is!" – "Oh no it isn't!" routine.

Cinderella at The Townhouse Theatre!

Book early for this year's spectacular pantomime and bring all the family…

If you're in England this winter, "Look Behind you!"

The lights go down, the audience falls silent. Suddenly, there's billowing smoke and a "baddie" rather like a nasty red devil emerges from the left, the sinister side of the stage. The baddie sneers and curses the characters we're about to meet, listing the awful things he'd like to happen to them.

"Not so fast," says a beautiful fairy, drifting onto the stage (in a harness) from above and waving her sparkly wand. Little girls gasp at her costume and the adults are comforted – good will once more triumph over evil.

And another pantomime has begun! Another generation of children is being drawn into the fantastic, hilarious and sometimes very naughty world of this very English holiday entertainment.

Pantomime is full of stock characters, none of whom can be omitted because pantomime-goers expect to see a romantic couple in the form of a beautiful maiden or princess and a "principal boy", who's actually a girl in tights, playing the hero. And there has to be a pantomime dame! The dame, probably the best-loved character of all, is always played by a man in show-stopping, outrageous dresses!

Pantomimes are based on traditional fairy tales. Take *Aladdin*, which features the lamp-discovering boy (played by a woman, of course), a lovely princess, the wicked uncle and Aladdin's mother, Widow Twanky (the dame), who runs a laundry and has been a favourite for centuries. Other popular stories are *Cinderella, Jack and the Beanstalk* and *Snow White, Sleeping Beauty* and *Babes in the Wood*.

One of the earliest pantomimes was *Robinson Crusoe*. This show, which first played in 1778 at the Theatre Royal, Drury Lane in London, wove in stock characters from Italian Commedia dell'arte: Harlequin, Columbine and the clown Pantaloon (introduced to British audiences more than 100 years earlier), with the shipwrecked mariner Crusoe and his companion, Man Friday. This mixture of characters with a British-based plotline established the foundation for stock characters.

The 1778 production, incidentally, included a young actor called Joseph Grimaldi, who specialised in the spectacle of pantomime. Grimaldi became the most famous of pantomime clowns, pioneering the art of the cross-dressing dame with such characters as Queen Rondabellyana.

Pantomime is family entertainment, but it's not just aimed at kids. It's full of topical, political allusions and suggestive comments, which may be rude, but never offensive or abusive. If you want to experience English pantomime for yourself, you'll find professional and amateur productions in just about every town during the winter season. So, if you're planning a winter trip to England, make sure to take in this historical entertainment. It's fun!

Section A: Directed Writing

1. Imagine you are an American planning to visit family in Britain. You have read about English pantomimes and would like to take your seven-year-old British nephew Simon and his twin sister Sofia to see *Cinderella* in London.

   Write a letter to the children's parents asking permission to take them to the pantomime. Tell them what the children will see and why you think they will enjoy it. Add any other details you consider to be relevant. Write between 250 and 350 words. Up to 15 marks are available for the content of your answer, and up to 25 marks for the quality of your writing. Start like this:

   Dear Jonas and Trudy,

   I'm coming to England in December and...

   Use a separate sheet of paper if necessary.

   ....
   ....
   ....
   ....
   ....
   ....
   ....
   ....
   ....
   ....
   ....
   ....
   ....
   ....
   ....
   ....
   ....
   ....
   ....
   ....
   ....
   ....
   ....
   ....
   ....

Section B: Composition

Write between 350 and 450 words on one of the following questions.

2. **Descriptive writing**

    a. Describe a crowded room at a birthday celebration.

    b. Describe a place of refuge or safe retreat.

    OR

3. **Narrative writing**

    a. Write a story that includes the words "I don't believe it".

    b. Write a story in which a character is in danger and time is running out.

    Use a separate sheet of paper if necessary.

....
....
....
....
....
....
....
....
....
....
....
....
....
....
....
....
....
....
....
....
....
....
....